THOROUGHBRED
Legends®

Affirmed
AND Alydar

Racing's Greatest Rivalry

TIMOTHY T. CAPPS

ECLIPSE
PRESS

Essex, Connecticut

ECLIPSE PRESS

An imprint of Globe Pequot, the trade division of
The Rowman & Littlefield Publishing Group, Inc.
4501 Forbes Blvd., Ste. 200
Lanham, MD 20706
www.rowman.com

Distributed by NATIONAL BOOK NETWORK

British Library Cataloguing in Publication Information available

Library of Congress Cataloging-in-Publication Data available

ISBN 978-1-4930-7695-6 (paper : alk. paper)
ISBN 978-1-4930-7894-3 (electronic)

∞™ The paper used in this publication meets the minimum requirements
of American National Standard for Information Sciences—Permanence of
Paper for Printed Library Materials, ANSI/NISO Z39.48-1992.

AFFIRMED & ALYDAR

CONTENTS

INTRODUCTION

Greatness On Display

There were 65,417 persons at Belmont Park on Saturday, June 10, 1978, each waiting to see whether Affirmed could become the eleventh American Triple Crown winner, the third of the decade, Secretariat (1973) and Seattle Slew (1977) having previously swept U.S. racing's most meaningful triad.

When the starting gate opened at 5:43 p.m. for the 110th running of the Belmont Stakes, the final leg of the "Triple," no one in the vast crowd could have been prepared for what he or she was about to see. A little less than two and a half minutes later, 2:26 4/5 to be precise, all 65,417 would be waiting for their pounding hearts to slow while acknowledging they would never again see a better horse race.

If young Thoroughbreds could watch films on how to race, the 1978 Belmont would be prime instruction

— it was that spectacular.

Affirmed, winner of the Kentucky Derby and Preakness, came into the Belmont with thirteen wins in fifteen career starts and more than one million dollars in earnings. He would go off as a well-deserved 3-5 favorite in the five-horse field.

His chief rival, for the ninth time in their young careers, would be Alydar. A splendid talent in his own right, Alydar was good enough to have been slightly favored over Affirmed in the Kentucky Derby, although he had only beaten the latter twice in their six meetings prior to the Derby.

Affirmed won the Derby by one and a half lengths over a late-running Alydar, then outdueled him by a neck after a stretch-long drive in the Preakness. By now, America's racing fans not only were enthralled by this spirited competition between two clearly exceptional colts, but were also firmly divided into Affirmed or Alydar camps.

Affirmed, perhaps because he had prepped for the Triple Crown in California, was identified as the Western hopeful, while Alydar was the quintessential "Eastern Establishment" horse, in no small part due to his being a product of the most fabled American racing and breeding empire, Calumet Farm.

Adding drama to the Belmont build-up was the belief on the part of a significant number of observers that Alydar might just have a slight advantage over his antagonist over the one and a half-mile distance of the Belmont, although nothing in either of their respective pedigrees or running styles suggested such an interpretation.

Such was the passion of the two horses' advocates that they would grasp at any straw, however speculative or flimsy, to justify their belief in their favorite's superiority.

Moreover, powerful finishers coming from well behind rarely win the Belmont, despite its length. Precisely because the race is so long, riders try to establish forward position, then conserve energy until that final long, sweeping turn into the stretch. The Belmont is a race in which tactical speed is particularly useful, and Affirmed had, more than Alydar, demonstrated both the ability to relax on the lead or behind horses and to provide quick bursts of acceleration when asked.

For Alydar to topple his archrival at Belmont, he would have to stay close to Affirmed in the early part of the race and then try to out-game or out-stay him in the long drive home. Tactically, at least, this figured to be the most interesting match between the two young-sters thus far.

Both colts had come out of their Derby-Preakness battles in good health, maintaining their weight and coat color well, and neither was allowed to relax between the Preakness and Belmont, especially Alydar.

Affirmed, typically an average work horse, was sent a mile in 1:40 1/5 by trainer Laz Barrera on June 1, then sailed through five furlongs in 1:01 on Wednesday, June 7, three days before his would-be coronation.

Trainer John Veitch, knowing Alydar would have to be on his toes earlier than usual in this race, worked the son of Raise a Native the full mile and a half of the Belmont, an unusual move, on June 1 (he got the trip in 2:43 3/5). On June 5 Alydar zipped six furlongs in 1:12 3/5, then breezed three furlongs in :35 the morning before the race.

Additionally, Veitch decided that for the first time since July of his two-year-old season, Alydar would race without blinkers. The trainer first put the shades on his colt because he wanted to tone down Alydar's early-race aggressiveness, but said he believed the colt was now mature enough to race without them.

While this seemed a risky choice given the stakes involved, it underscored Veitch's recognition of the need to adopt more forceful tactics against Affirmed.

Three other starters lined up to face the two aces — Darby Creek Road, Noon Time Spender, and Judge Advocate — but they were there to pick up the minor purse money and be footnotes to history.

Alydar and veteran jockey Jorge Velasquez drew post-position two while Affirmed and eighteen-year-old superstar rider Steve Cauthen were alongside in the three hole.

Barrera knew Alydar would be in the hunt early this day, so he told Cauthen to send Affirmed along from the start and try to get inside position. Affirmed did his expected duty and was in front by a length over Judge Advocate after a quarter-mile, with Alydar third, another one and a half lengths back. The latter got away smoothly, if unhurried, and settled into his rhythm during the first three furlongs. Then Velasquez, sensing the pace was too pedestrian (the first quarter in

:25 with no speed-up in sight), leveled off on his mount and went after the leader, who was bopping along at a relaxed clip a few feet off the inside rail.

Velasquez had Alydar in gear when they hit the one-mile marker, and track announcer Chic Anderson dramatically called, "Affirmed and Alydar are side by side with a mile to go," bringing a roar from the Alydar partisans who had been urging Velasquez to go after Affirmed.

The expected duel was now joined. But no onlooker could have been prepared for what was to follow. For the next 1:36 4/5 seconds, these superb equine athletes would match strides, with Affirmed holding the slightest of advantages, but never appearing to gain winning momentum.

They ran the third quarter in :24, the fourth quarter in :23 2/5, and the fifth quarter (on the final turn) in :24 1/5, all the time maintaining their perfect team relationship.

By the time the pair turned into the Belmont stretch, the crowd reached a crescendo. The two horses were painting a masterpiece, and those witnessing it were well aware they were present at its creation.

Despite Affirmed's steady drumbeat pace, Alydar relentlessly pursued him alongside, and in early stretch he appeared slightly the stronger of the two. The war of attrition was working.

Or was it?

With both riders low and driving, Alydar inched closer, and pushed somewhat ahead of Affirmed with about a furlong to go. The crowd, already in a frenzy, became delirious; Belmont Park had never been louder.

Cauthen, forced by the close proximity of the two colts to switch his whip to his left hand, pushed Affirmed back to level terms, and they streaked toward the wire evenly, tiring but unrelenting. Inside the last fifty yards, Affirmed edged ahead by inches, but Alydar would surge one last time, drawing even again. Could his momentum get him to the lead once more, at the climactic moment? Driving straight and true, every muscle straining, the two chestnuts reached for the finish line. Alydar was unwavering, unflinching, but so was the Derby-Preakness winner.

Then, it was over, and Affirmed had gotten his head in front, winner by about a foot. After one and a half miles — 2,640 yards, 7,920 feet — Affirmed was better, by a foot.

Two horses, two jockeys, and 65,417 spectators were exhausted. Affirmed had won his Triple Crown, and none of his predecessors had worked as hard, or shown more gallantry, in their bids for classic glory. Alydar, too, had earned his place in Triple Crown lore as the first horse ever to finish second in all three races and the endless respect of a generation of racing fans and horsemen.

The greatest Belmont ever? The greatest race anybody ever saw? Who knew and who cared, for this was a mesmerizing moment, two and a half minutes of exhilaration and accomplishment. Two magnificent Thoroughbreds had raced into immortality, and they took everyone who shared the experience along for the ride.

If there had been a message board in Belmont's infield that day, it would have read, "Greatness was on display, times two." It was as good as horse racing gets.

Timothy T. Capps

Columbia, Maryland 2001

CHAPTER 1

Bred To Win

The memorable horses of Thoroughbred history can emerge from anywhere, of course, but Affirmed and Alydar were products of two highly successful breeding and racing operations, both accustomed to playing the game at high levels and routinely visiting the sport's most hallowed winner's circles.

Affirmed was a Florida-bred, foaled and raised at his owner's Harbor View Farm near Ocala. That owner, Louis E. Wolfson, was a Floridian himself, and a man who adopted success as a lifestyle at an early age. Growing up in Jacksonville, Florida, in the 1920s, he was a four-sport star athlete in high school, then headed off to the University of Georgia to play football.

He became a starter as a sophomore but suffered a career-ending shoulder injury while tackling Yale University legend Albie Booth in 1931. He stayed in

Athens an additional year, playing basketball and wrestling, but eventually dropped out to work with his father in the latter's scrap metal business.

The young Wolfson helped his father rescue the family business by the mid-1930s, then parlayed that experience and a shrewd understanding of the use of leverage into a business empire that made him one of the American business community's most admired — and feared — figures.

Wolfson was a "conglomerateer" before most people knew the term. He bought and sold companies, engaged in proxy fights and stock maneuvers at a bewildering pace, and challenged corporate managers to perform or be sent packing. Gaining control of Merritt-Chapman & Scott, a multi-line industrial holding company, he made millions of dollars for himself and shareholders. He made a few enemies as well.

Wolfson's fast-paced merger and acquisition activity, while making him the object of cover stories of the nation's leading business publications, also caught the attention of the U.S. Securities and Exchange Commission. The SEC charged Wolfson with violations of Rule 144, the selling of so-called "letter stock," the unregistered stock that is typically distributed to corporate insiders when a company makes a public stock offering.

Such stock has to be held for a certain minimum period before it can be sold, and there are stiff civil penalties for premature sale of unregistered securities. The SEC claimed Wolfson had breached its letter stock regulations; he said he had not done so; and the courts were handed the case to decide.

Wolfson lost his SEC fight, but he pursued exoneration for many years, believing that his business enemies had targeted him because of his unorthodox "new era" approach to corporate finance.

On the racing front, Wolfson moved as quickly from beginner to head of the class as he had in business. A horseplayer for many years, Wolfson bought his first racehorses privately in 1958 and was in action at the Keeneland July yearling sale that same year, buying four yearlings for $114,000.

Among those youngsters was Francis S., a son of the Nearco stallion Royal Charger, who would go on to become a major New York stakes winner. By 1960 Harbor View Farm, as Wolfson called his outfit, was showing off its pink-and-black silks on so many quality horses that the stable finished third nationally in earnings, beginning an eight-year run in the top ten.

This amazingly quick success included some high-class horses, such as Garwol, Roving Minstrel, Wolfram, Stevward, Irvkup, and, in 1963, a flaming comet named Raise a Native. Purchased as a yearling in 1962 at Saratoga for $39,000, the son of the mighty Native Dancer and the Case Ace mare Raise You was a marvelous specimen of his breed, a powerful and commanding presence as a two-year-old.

The imposing chestnut was so startlingly impressive in his first four starts at two, setting or equaling three track records while disdaining his opposition, that he seemed virtually invincible.

Raise a Native was being compared to his own sire, to Citation, Count Fleet, even Man o' War. The colt's trainer, the veteran Burley Parke, who had been coaxed out of retirement by Wolfson, thought he was "the greatest young horse I've ever trained," the horse of a lifetime. On the morning of August 2, 1963, while Raise a Native prepared for the Sapling Stakes at Monmouth Park, all those comparisons ended abruptly when he ruptured a tendon sheath on his left foreleg.

Parke and many others were crushed by Raise a Native's sudden disappearance from the racetrack, but Wolfson, by then knee-deep in the breeding business with more than a hundred broodmares, accepted this setback with equanimity, sending the colt off to stud at Spendthrift Farm in Kentucky, where the son of Native Dancer would be instantly popular with breeders.

Wolfson had other good ones in the barn, including a compact gelding named Roman Brother, who had neither Raise a Native's physical presence nor his high turn of speed. Roman Brother was durable, however, and he improved so steadily that in 1965 he was able to grab a piece of the Horse of the Year title.

By that time, Raise a Native's first offspring were on the ground, and his small first crop of eleven foals contained four future stakes winners, among them a Harbor View-bred and -owned youngster out of the superior broodmare Exclusive.

A sleek chestnut named Exclusive Native, the colt was a top-notch two-year-old. He won his first three starts, including Saratoga's Sanford Stakes, and then ran well, but not well enough to win, in four consecutive major stakes, the last one in the Futurity at Belmont. He suffered a slight cannon bone fracture in the Futurity and was away from the races until the following summer, when he returned to win the Arlington Classic. He came out of his next start, the Monmouth Invitational, worse than he went in and was sent to Spendthrift to begin stud duties alongside his sire.

Wolfson, in the midst of his legal battles with the SEC, briefly stopped racing, although his breeding operation continued unabated. He was soon back in the saddle, so to speak, in the early seventies, campaigning high-profile horses such as Native Royalty, Raisela, Princely Native, Due Diligence, Affiliate, and the early Exclusive Natives such as Root Cause and Life's Hope.

Harbor View Farm led the nation's breeders by earnings in 1970 and '71, and the racing stable was soon back on the top ten owners list.

Wolfson had been widowed for several years when he married Patrice Jacobs, daughter of training legend Hirsch Jacobs, in 1972. She would become not only his lifelong companion, but also an adviser in breeding matters, a circumstance that would become critical in the making of a racing superstar. Meanwhile, Wolfson, having decided his Thoroughbred empire had gotten a bit unwieldy, was culling his broodmare band to manageable size. He also began planning to sell the Harbor View Farm property, which he would do in late 1977, moving many of his mares and young horses to nearby Happy Valley Farm, owned and operated by his sons, Gary and Steve.

That this reduction would occur just as Wolfson was on the verge of his greatest racing triumphs was as improbable as its coincidence with a resurgence in fortunes of one of the great franchise names in American sports.

While there is always room to argue over the "golden age" of horse racing in America, there can be little doubt that the 1940s and early '50s saw the sport reach unimagined levels of popularity and business growth.

Playing no small part in making Thoroughbred racing's story a prominent one was the incredible success of Calumet Farm, the Lexington, Kentucky-based breeding establishment.

Calumet, named for the baking powder company owned by founder William Monroe Wright, was originally a Standardbred farm, and a successful one, producing Calumet Butler, winner of trotting's Kentucky

Derby equivalent, the Hambletonian, in 1931, the year the elder Wright passed away.

His son, Warren Wright Sr., was more interested in Thoroughbreds than Standardbreds, and he began dispersing the latter while acquiring the former.

Warren Wright launched his Thoroughbred activities by acquiring good racemares, which he believed were essential to a consistently productive breeding program, while buying yearlings for his racing stable and cultivating relationships with the leading stallion managers of the day.

In 1936 Wright was part of a syndicate put together by A.B. Hancock Sr. to purchase English Derby winner and promising young sire Blenheim II (his son Mahmoud won that year's English Derby) to stand at Hancock's Claiborne Farm. Blenheim was also a son of the world's leading classic sire of that era, Blandford, and Wright, who owned a quarter of the shares, was eager to cross him with the best American lines, especially those noted for speed and durability.

That same year at Saratoga, Wright spent $14,000 to buy a yearling by Bull Dog out of the Ballot mare Rose Leaves. Named Bull Lea, he became a good, but not special, racehorse, excelling over middle distances without appearing to be quite top-class.

His stud credentials did not seem especially promising, other than his opportunity to be bred to members of the fast-burgeoning and qualitatively strong Calumet broodmare band.

However, if expectations for Bull Lea had been high, he would have exceeded them. From his first crop (foals of 1941) onward, not only was he sensational, he was to become the dominant sire of the forties and fifties.

He would sire a Triple Crown winner (Citation), three Kentucky Derby winners, and nine champions; lead the North American general sire list five times; and get fifty-eight stakes winners from 377 foals, an excellent fifteen percent.

Bull Lea had advantages, of course, such as being part of a well-managed farm operation, having access to what was almost certainly the best privately held broodmare band in the United States at the time, and the good fortune of having many of his progeny placed into the care of an incomparable horseman, Ben Jones.

Still, the sire lists of history are littered with well-bred, high-class runners that had terrific opportunities and could not convert them. Bull Lea did so, and his stallion power, combined with a determined use of Wright's ample resources to maintain a large and high-quality group of mares and Jones' skills as an evaluator and conditioner of horses, proved to be an epochal example of the right people — and horses — in the right place at the right time.

Beginning in 1940, Jones' first full year as trainer, Calumet was in the top-ten owners' list for twenty-two consecutive years, finishing as low as tenth only once, leading the list twelve times, finishing second four times and third twice.

Bull Lea's progeny were so good that Jones advised Wright and his wife, Lucille, who inherited Calumet when Wright died in 1950, not to breed him to many outside mares.

Calumet did so to a great extent, as well as using Blenheim II. This approach meant fewer opportunities for the many good males the racing stable was producing, such as Triple Crown winner Whirlaway, Derby and Preakness winner Pensive, Preakness winner Faultless, Horse of the Year Coaltown, Derby winner Ponder, Derby winner Hill Gail, multiple major stakes winner

Mark-Ye-Well, Derby winner Iron Liege, champion and dual classic winner Tim Tam, and, of course, Citation.

All the great Calumet racemares likewise presented problems because many were by Bull Lea and could not be bred to his sons or grandsons readily, so Calumet had to rely on outside stallions, which typically reduces the percentages of success for private breeders.

Thus, it was not surprising that as Bull Lea aged, and none of his sons — perhaps because of limited opportunities — were good sires, the farm's fortunes declined.

Calumet fell far out of the top ten in stable earnings in the early sixties (Bull Lea died at age twenty-nine in 1964) and did not return until 1968 when Forward Pass won the Derby and Preakness. Horses such as Best Turn, Eastern Fleet, and Gleaming would lead another brief resurgence in the early seventies, but Calumet's fall from the throne room of American racing had been so sudden as to be shocking.

Lucille Wright, now married to Rear Admiral Gene Markey, had gradually reduced the scope of the Calumet breeding operation as Bull Lea faded and it became evident there were no replacements on the horizon.

By the mid-seventies the Calumet broodmare band

typically numbered in the high twenties, compared to the eighties during the farm's salad years, and the farm stallions consisted of Best Turn, a Turn-to horse; Gleaming, by Herbager; and Raise a Cup, a son of Raise a Native; all home-bred and raced.

The great Calumet female families were still around, though, especially the wonderful tribe of Blue Delight, and the farm's use of outside stallions had increased, perhaps setting the stage for another run at glory. Hints that this might be the case came with the emergence of a daughter of Herbager and Sweet Tooth, herself a great-granddaughter of Blue Delight. The filly's name was Our Mims, and she would win the Coaching Club American Oaks on her way to champion three-year-old filly honors. But there was more — much more — just off stage.

CHAPTER 2

Common Denominators

G reat horses are both born and made, and while the making part usually has more dramatic human stories attached to it, the rest of the story is often as compelling because racehorses are the only athletes with planned parentages, the products of generations of designer matings.

Affirmed and Alydar were among the 28,271 foals born in 1975, the vast majority of which would be destined for racing mediocrity, if that. Slightly more than three percent of any foal crop will win stakes races, and perhaps one percent will win graded stakes, racing's elite contests.

A handful — generally fewer than ten — will go on to win year-end championships, and an occasional horse will emerge as a champion in successive years, perhaps even seizing the imagination enough to be labeled as great. If bestowal of greatness sounds somewhat random, it is, and that is the ultimate mystery — and challenge — of the world's oldest spectator sport.

How do you breed greatness? No one really knows, although thousands of hours are spent annually poring over pedigrees and race records, looking for the key that would unlock the great pedigree puzzle. Some foals, of course, are born with better opportunities than others, based on pedigrees, connections, quality of upbringing, etc.

Affirmed and Alydar were certainly among those favored foals of the class of 1975. Both came from top-notch private breeding establishments, each was raised under optimum conditions and sent to established trainers, and both had pedigrees suggesting they could be good ones.

Interestingly, they had a meaningful family link that made them blood relations. In addition, their exploits established their male line as an international force. That link was, of course, the aforementioned Raise a Native, sire of Alydar, paternal grandsire of Affirmed.

Raise a Native's racing career, as recounted previously, was brilliant and brief. He made his first appearance at Hialeah on February 28, 1963, in one of those three-furlong "baby" races typical of American winter racing at that time.

His early morning work had drawn enough attention to earn him favoritism among the fourteen starters in what amounted to a Quarter Horse cavalry charge down the Hialeah homestretch. Raise a Native, hauling jockey John Rotz, ran away from his field by six lengths in the time of :33 2/5 seconds.

Burley Parke, who had trained multiple Futurity winners Occupation and Occupy, in addition to stars such as Blue Delight, Errard, Free For All, and champion Noor, knew young talent when he saw it, and he recognized uncommon ability in the strapping chestnut son of Native Dancer.

The trainer returned Raise a Native to the races on May 4 at Aqueduct in a five-furlong allowance race, which the colt won by eight lengths in :57 4/5, breaking the track record for the distance.

On May 31 Raise a Native was under starter's orders again, this time in the Juvenile Stakes at Aqueduct, and he dispatched his five antagonists — and the teletimer — with ease, winning by two and a half lengths in a record-equaling :57 4/5 for five furlongs.

His next start would come almost seven weeks later in the five and a half-furlong Great American Stakes at Aqueduct, where he would face only three foes, albeit one of them Chieftain, a dual stakes-winning son of the great sire Bold Ruler.

Raise a Native thoroughly dominated the Great American, rolling through the first quarter-mile in :21 3/5, the half in :44 1/5, and five furlongs in :56 2/5. Under a hand ride from jockey Manuel Ycaza, Raise a Native extended a one-length margin over his only challenger, Mr. Brick, at the eighth pole, to two at the wire. The final time of 1:02 3/5 set a new track record by one and one-fifth seconds.

His high cruising rate brought gasps of admiration from onlookers, but also raised questions about his ability to carry such speed over longer distances. Raise a Native's speed was evident, and his pedigree suggested that middle distances, at least, should be well within his realm. The questions were: would he let himself "go long"? Could he be rated?

His next target was Monmouth Park's Sapling Stakes over six furlongs on August 3. While breezing over the Monmouth surface the morning before the race, Raise a Native ruptured the tendon sheath on his left foreleg, ending his racing career far too early and leaving unanswered questions of distance capacity, versatility, and ultimate class.

Breeders had seen enough, though, to assure him of excellent patronage from the start of his stud career in 1964. His brilliant precocity and a pedigree that presented an interesting mix of inbreeding and outcrossing were sufficient to make him one of the most intriguing young stallion prospects around.

Raise a Native's male line was yet another branch of the mighty Phalaris tribe, this one descending through Phalaris' son Sickle.

Phalaris is rightfully regarded as one of the most influential stallions in Thoroughbred history, with his male-line descendants now accounting for more than ninety percent of stakes winners in the world each year.

He came from the "wrong" branch of the male line of 1880 English Derby winner Bend Or, who was a superbly made horse of high class and bad forelegs and a wonderful stallion. Bend Or would sire the unbeaten Ormonde, whose male line would remain vital through Teddy and his offspring, and who would figure prominently in the pedigrees of Affirmed and Alydar.

Another son of Bend Or was the miler Bona Vista, who won the Two Thousand Guineas and was half brother to two top-class horses. Bona Vista went to stud confronted with modest expectations, but managed to sire Cyllene before being sold for stallion duty to a breeder in Hungary, where he would become a foundation stallion.

Cyllene would prove to be a standout racer, though not nominated to the classics. He was an even better sire, leading the English sire list twice and leaving behind four Derby winners.

Leaving behind is the correct term, because Cyllene was sold for stud duty to a farm in Argentina when he was thirteen and became an important stallion there.

His most meaningful contribution to the breed came not from his Derby-winning sons, but from a colt who won his share of good races yet appeared to be well below classic form. His name was Polymelus, and if his race record was spotty, his stud record was not. He was England's leading sire five times, getting four classic winners and the champion sprinter Phalaris.

The latter won over longer distances but in top company was at his best over sprint distances, where he was almost unbeatable. At stud Phalaris outdid himself, siring numerous high-class horses that stayed better than he and, more importantly, embellished his male line further with each succeeding generation.

Today almost every male line of consequence traces to Lord Derby's good sprinter, a tribute to his ability to pass on his speed, durability, and versatility to his offspring and beyond.

One of Phalaris' best-bred sons was Sickle, the first foal of the good racemare Selene, a tiny filly who won sixteen of her twenty-two starts, from sprints to one and three-quarters miles in quality company.

Sickle was a good two-year-old, rated third best of his generation, and was a strong third in the Two Thousand Guineas in 1927, but ended his career with an unplaced finish in the Derby. He started his reproductive career in England at his owner's (Lord Derby) stud and then was leased to prominent American breeder-owner Joseph E. Widener, who had purchased the legendary Elmendorf Farm near Lexington, Kentucky, and was building his stallion roster.

Sickle became a success at Elmendorf, and Widener

exercised his purchase option in 1932. Sickle went on to lead the North American sire list twice and sire forty-three stakes winners. Among them was Unbreakable, whom Widener sent to England to race, perhaps because both sides of the colt's pedigree were very British.

Like his sire, Unbreakable was a good juvenile who had less success at three. He was clearly happiest at sprint distances, never winning past a mile in a fourteen-race career. Thus, the pattern continued from Polymelus through Phalaris, Sickle, and Unbreakable — early maturity, good speed, limited distance capacity.

Unbreakable was a moderate stallion at Elmendorf, siring thirteen stakes winners, but he did his part to improve the breed through the horse who was by far his best, Polynesian.

That colt, given to Mrs. P.A.B. Widener II by her husband (whose father bred the colt) as a wedding anniversary gift, would prove to have lasting value.

Polynesian was a solid two-year-old, especially at Pimlico where he won the Sagamore Stakes, but he was better at three when he won the Withers, the Preakness, and two other stakes races.

At four he started a remarkable twenty times over

various distances, winning eight races and finishing second or third eight times. He ran six furlongs in 1:08 4/5 in the Roseben Handicap down Belmont's Widener Chute and equaled the world record for six furlongs around a turn by running 1:09 1/5 in the Pageant Handicap at Atlantic City. He was competitive over longer distances, winning the Riggs Handicap at Pimlico over one and three-sixteenths miles, but was clearly a force at a mile or less.

At five he won nine of fourteen races, always carrying weights in the high-120s to mid-130s. He won under 134 pounds; took the Camden Handicap at Garden State under 129 in 1:09 4/5, a six-furlong track record; beat Armed in a sprint at Belmont Park; and finished his career with a one-length win over the speedy The Doge while carrying 134 pounds in Pimlico's Janney Handicap.

Polynesian was good-looking, interestingly bred (inbred 4x3 to Polymelus), and possessed of high-end speed, exceptional durability, and good racing character. At stud he was underrated, siring thirty-seven stakes winners, among them Imbros, Barbizon, Alanesian, and Mommy Dear.

He will, however, be forever remembered as the sire of Native Dancer.

The writer asked Alfred Vanderbilt, breeder and owner of Native Dancer, not long before his death why he chose Polynesian as a mate for his Discovery mare Geisha.

Vanderbilt thought for a second and then said, "He was a good outcross for her, and I felt he was one of the best racehorses I saw in the 1940s." Vanderbilt went on to say that he believed Polynesian with better management would have had a much more impressive race record.

Whatever the merit of Vanderbilt's viewpoint, the mating of Polynesian and Geisha was magical. Geisha was by Discovery, the iron horse campaigned by Vanderbilt in the 1930s. He was a great weight carrier and thoroughly tough and versatile performer. Geisha was only a fair racehorse, but she was out of the stakes winner Miyako, a half sister to stakes winner Planetoid (dam of the monumental broodmare Grey Flight) and full sister to the champion two-year-old of 1938, El Chico.

This was a precocious family, inbred to the outstanding American sire Ben Brush, thus making its female members prime candidates for matings with stouter male lines, such as that of Discovery.

The result was a big gray colt whose genetic blend of speed and stamina, precocity, and tractability was almost perfection.

Native Dancer was a major-league racehorse from his first start in April of 1952 through his last effort at Saratoga in August of 1954.

He was nine for nine as a two-year-old, including four stakes wins at Saratoga (the Flash, Saratoga Special, Grand Union Hotel, and Hopeful) and a world-record performance in Belmont's Futurity Stakes (six and a half furlongs on a straight course in 1:14 2/5).

He only raced farther than six and a half furlongs once (one and one-sixteenth miles in his final juvenile start) but was so dominant that most observers were all but conceding the 1953 Triple Crown to him. Man o' War and Citation were the names being mentioned in conjunction with Native Dancer. He was given the unusually high weight of 130 pounds on the Experimental Free Handicap, a weighting of the previous year's juveniles based on two races to be run in the spring in New York (the races were discontinued in the 1950s) but viewed more widely as an early evaluation of the merits of that year's classic contenders. Native Dancer was weighted seven pounds more than the next horses, Laffango and Tahitian King, who were assigned 123. The seven-pound spread from the highweight to the second highweight was the largest in the history of the Free Handicap, a further testimonial to the impression Native Dancer made at two.

The colt had bucked his shins in the summer of 1952, not that this troubled his march through the two-year-old ranks in late summer and fall, and he had had osselets (bony growths in the ankles) that were treated with a blistering agent in California, where he wintered prior to his three-year-old season.

Native Dancer won the Gotham Stakes and Wood Memorial in preparation for the Kentucky Derby. He lost his first and only race in one of the most talked-about Derbys in history. Bumped on the first turn and checked, then held up slightly coming out of the final turn, he got free to chase down the pacesetting Dark Star in early stretch.

He reduced the margin steadily and made one final rush just before the wire, but fell short by a head. His jockey, Eric Guerin, was widely criticized for his all-around bad judgment, although some said the Dancer had a fair shot and just couldn't get the job done.

The speculation was entertaining but fruitless, for Native Dancer won the Preakness (Dark Star bowed a tendon while leading) and Belmont (running one and a half miles in 2:28 3/5, equaling the second-fastest time ever for the Belmont), then took the Dwyer Stakes, Arlington Classic, Travers Stakes, and the American Derby in succession.

Bruises in his left front foot were treated after the American Derby, and he sat out the rest of 1953.

As a four-year-old, Native Dancer won an allowance race at Belmont under 126 pounds, then packed 130 pounds in the one-turn, one-mile Metropolitan Handicap. He relaxed at the back of the field going down the backstretch to such a degree that at the head of the stretch he had seven lengths to make up on the leader, Greentree Stable's star gelding, Straight Face.

Relentlessly, he surged forward under Guerin, catching Straight Face yards before the wire to win by a neck in 1:35 1/5, his own final quarter run in just over twenty-three seconds.

His ankle problems flared up again and he raced only once more, winning the seven-furlong Oneonta

Handicap at Saratoga by nine lengths under 137 pounds.

He went to stud at Vanderbilt's Sagamore Farm in Maryland with a record of twenty-one wins in twenty-two starts, a head short of perfect. While there were those who said his competition was lacking, no exception could be taken to his style and his imposing appearance. He had great speed, the ability to carry it over classic distances, and a commanding presence.

His pedigree was an interesting blend of American and European speed and stamina, and black-and-white television had made him into a star, a household name to a greater degree than any other horse since Man o' War.

A stud fee of $15,000 was set, a big number for 1955, but there was no shortage of applicants for seasons, and Vanderbilt could be selective in his choice of mates.

Native Dancer was certainly the best horse in his direct male line since Bend Or, but great racehorses are often not great sires. In fact, Native Dancer got off to a relatively slow and perhaps disappointing start, his best early progeny being European.

By the early 1960s, though, he was on a roll. At the time of his premature death at age seventeen, he had established himself as a world-class stallion. In addition to twin classic winner Kauai King and disqualified Kentucky Derby winner Dancer's Image, Native Dancer sired French classic-placed Dan Cupid, himself sire of Sea-Bird, regarded as Europe's best racehorse of the twentieth century.

An obscure Native Dancer colt named Atan, a foal of 1961 as was Raise a Native, would prove to be key to the emergence of Native Dancer's sire line abroad. Winner of his only start, Atan stood in England for a modest stud fee and sired only four stakes winners, one of which was Sharpen Up, a quality runner who became a superb — and versatile — sire.

Sharpen Up sired eighty-three stakes winners, including champion filly Pebbles, Prix de l'Arc de Triomphe winner Trempolino, ace milers Kris and Selkirk, juvenile star Diesis, and the crack sprinter Sharpo.

Kris, Diesis, and Selkirk have all done well at stud, and their branch of the Native Dancer line seems assured of a place of prominence in the foreseeable future.

Raise a Native, meanwhile, got off to a predictably fast start, his early crops exhibiting the expected precocious speed, along with some expected soundness issues.

A member of his second crop, a gorgeous chestnut

colt out of the Royal Charger mare Gay Hostess, was sold to Canadian Frank McMahon for $250,000 at the Keeneland July yearling sale in 1967.

Two years later, this gifted and gritty colt would win the first two legs of the Triple Crown while still unbeaten and finish second in the Belmont while not at his physical best. Majestic Prince's racing career and his subsequent stud career showed that Raise a Native was not a one-dimensional sire and that he would, as British bloodstock authority Tony Morris said in his book *Thoroughbred Stallions*, "spread class, speed and unsoundness, often as a package, among the Thoroughbred population."

Raise a Native's first crop was small, only eleven foals, and included Exclusive Native, whose own racing career was discussed previously. Exclusive Native was produced from a Vanderbilt-bred mare, Exclusive, herself a winning daughter of Shut Out, the 1942 Kentucky Derby and Belmont winner. There wasn't all that much in her family to recommend Exclusive as a broodmare, but she established herself as a legitimate star, producing stakes winners Exclusive Nashua, Irvkup, Mellow Marsh, Exclusive Dancer, and Exclusive

Native, the final four for Lou Wolfson after he bought her from Major Albert Warner, who had purchased her from Vanderbilt.

Her produce record earned her dates with Raise a Native, and Exclusive Native alone would easily justify Wolfson's decision to buy her and send her to the best horse he had owned.

By the time Affirmed and Alydar were foaled, Raise a Native was well established as the leading American influence for speed, although Bold Ruler was still the dominant force in American breeding with Northern Dancer and Hail to Reason also making their marks and American-breds forging to the forefront of European racing.

Raise a Native's sons were also starting to make their place in the world, especially Exclusive Native, whose first crop included the multiple stakes winner Our Native, a colt whose misfortune was to be born the same year as Secretariat, Sham, and Forego, but who had the class to win the Flamingo Stakes, Ohio Derby, and Monmouth Invitational (now the Haskell). Also a member of that crop of 1970 was a highly touted son of Raise a Native named Mr. Prospector, a sprinter whose racing career was compromised to some extent by physical problems. He would begin his stud career in Florida in 1975, and his first crop would reach the track in 1978, the year Affirmed and Alydar had the racing world's rapt attention.

The mare whose visit to Exclusive Native would result in Affirmed did not have the same apparent credentials as did Exclusive when she went to Raise a Native.

Bred and raced by F. Eugene Dixon, he a Widener on his maternal side, the mare in question was named Won't Tell You, and her race record, along with that of her dam and granddam, was more about durability than class. She started twenty-three times, mostly in claiming company, winning five starts. Her dam, Scarlet Ribbon, won five claimers in twenty-six career starts. The nearest black type was that of Billings, a good sort who chased Citation fruitlessly in 1948, and Royal Native, best older filly of 1960 and half sister to Won't Tell You's third dam.

The sire of Won't Tell You was Crafty Admiral, a horse now largely forgotten in pedigrees but a tough and talented racehorse who was America's champion handicapper of 1952 and just missed Horse of the Year honors.

Crafty Admiral was bred by Captain Harry Guggenheim at Claiborne Farm in 1948. A June foal, he was sold with Guggenheim's other yearlings the following year at a dispersal auction to Hugh Grant, with A.B. "Bull" Hancock Jr., who liked the colt, being the underbidder. Crafty Admiral showed some ability at two, then was sold again privately to Charles Cohen, who was buying his first-ever racehorse. As luck would have it to first-time owner Cohen would go the spoils.

Crafty Admiral would go postward sixteen times in 1952, winning nine races, including the Gulfstream Park Handicap (one and a quarter miles), Brooklyn Handicap (one and a quarter miles), the Merchants' and Citizens' Handicap (one and three-sixteenths miles), and the Washington Park Handicap (one mile). He was in the lead after a mile and a half in the two-mile Jockey Club Gold Cup, but was dusted in the stretch by three-year-olds One Count and Mark-Ye-Well.

A son of Fighting Fox, a capable racer and full brother to Gallant Fox, Crafty Admiral was a fast and genuine horse, versatile enough to sprint or go moderately long (ten furlongs was about his limit). Interestingly, he was inbred to the excellent French runner and sire Teddy through the full brothers Sir Gallahad III and Bull Dog. This cross would prove to be a matter of significance in the matings that produced both Affirmed and Alydar.

Wolfson bought Won't Tell You, in foal to Raise a Native, from Fitz Dixon for $18,000 at the 1972 Keeneland January sale, along with three other mares. He bought her primarily for her Raise a Native foal and the outcross she represented (no Phalaris blood), and she produced for him a Raise a Native colt, named Century Gold, who earned more than $48,000 before being claimed, and a Native Heritage colt who earned $11,600 before being claimed.

Her foals had earned back their dam's purchase price and more, but not a lot more. Barren in 1974, she was bred to Exclusive Native that year because Patrice Wolfson noted the doubling up of Teddy blood that would result from such a mating. (Raise a Native was out of Raise You, a daughter of the speedy Case Ace, an American-born son of Teddy; Crafty Admiral's paternal grandsire was Sir Gallahad III, a son of Teddy, and his second dam, Boola Brook, was by Sir Gallahad's full brother Bull Dog. Both Sir Gallahad III and Bull Dog raced in France, then compiled excellent sire records in the United States, with Bull Dog siring none other than Calumet Farm's great progenitor, Bull Lea.)

If Affirmed's female family was questionable, Alydar's was the opposite. Although Calumet, lacking a top-class home sire after the demise of Bull Lea, had fallen from its accustomed pedestal, its broodmare band of the 1970s was made up mostly of descendants of its powerful producers of the forties and fifties.

The bluest of the many Calumet blue hens, at least over the long haul, was Blue Delight, a multiple stakes winner for Chicago owner John Marsh. Warren Wright, who was always looking for quality race mares, purchased her after her racing career ended and bred her to Bull Lea. The result was a good stakes winner named All Blue, the first of nine foals Blue Delight would produce for Calumet and the first of five stakes winners.

Her best was the champion filly Real Delight, by Bull Lea, although she also produced Kentucky Oaks winner Bubbley and Princess Turia, the latter a competitive sort who would become the dam of Forward Pass.

Real Delight herself produced three stakes winners, among them the Ponder filly Plum Cake, who foaled stakes winners Sugar Plum Time and Plum Bold, both by Bold Ruler, and Yule Log, another Bold Ruler who produced 1982 three-year-old champion filly Christmas Past.

Plum Cake's most important baby, from Calumet's standpoint, was a complete homebred. Born in 1965, she was by On-and-On, a Calumet-bred by Nasrullah out of the Calumet champion mare Two Lea, another Bull Lea. Named Sweet Tooth, she was stakes-placed as a two-year-old, enough to earn her a place among the Calumet broodmares.

Her 1974 foal, a filly by Herbager named Our Mims, was named three-year-old champion filly in 1977, at the end of a season that saw her year-younger half brother, named Alydar, join her to elevate Calumet's racing stable back toward the top of the owners' tree.

Intriguingly, Alydar, like Affirmed a chestnut from the Raise a Native sire line, had even more crosses of Teddy, both from Raise a Native (Raise You, by Case Ace, by Teddy) and from Sweet Tooth (by On-and-On, a son of Two Lea by Bull Lea, by Bull Dog, by Teddy, and out of Plum Cake, a daughter of Real Delight, by Bull Lea, etc.).

Who and what was Teddy?

A French-bred from the great breeding operation of Edmond Blanc, Teddy had the misfortune to be a war baby, a foal of 1913 whose racing career was compromised by World War I. By the unbeaten Ajax, himself a son of English Triple Crown winner Flying Fox, out of a good race mare in Rondeau, Teddy raced at three, mostly in Spain, and won five of seven starts, although his form was hard to judge.

His one start at four, in the ten-furlong Prix de Sablonieres, was his most meaningful, because he defeated La Farina, one of the best French horses of the era.

Teddy at stud left no doubts about his class. He consistently got quality horses, such as Asterus, the great Italian star Ortello, Sir Gallahad III, Bull Dog (a moderate stakes winner but very good sire), and, in his old age in the United States, Case Ace and Sun Teddy. The latter would be the thread to the remaining male line branch of Teddy through his son, the aforementioned Calumet-bred Sun Again, who would establish a line running through Damascus.

Teddy sired sixty-five stakes winners (more than eighteen percent of his named foals, an extraordinary percentage), and he was the consummate sire of middle-distance class.

How much did Teddy's multiple presences lend to the pedigrees and racing characters of Affirmed and Alydar? That is the unsolved riddle of bloodstock breeding, but for those who believe in inbreeding to superior individuals, the connection is there and it is significant.

CHAPTER 3

Young Guns

T wo-year-old racing has undergone numerous transformations during roughly a century and a half of experimentation.

Before winter racing in Southern climes flourished, two-year-olds usually got started in late spring in three- or four-furlong dashes that amounted to a little more than exhibitions for the sake of experience. Those would be followed by the normal run of conditional allowances and stakes for the better ones, claimers for the rest, run over sprint distances up to, but rarely exceeding, seven furlongs or a mile.

The season for juveniles was usually over by October or early November when everyone packed up and headed South or to a farm or training center for the winter.

Eventually the popularity of winter racing at Hialeah, Santa Anita, and Fair Grounds led to earlier two-year-old races, most of them being the three-furlong variety. Increases in racing dates in other areas led to longer seasons, hence later two-year-old racing and added distances.

By the 1970s concerns about over-racing two-year-olds led many tracks to curtail or even eliminate winter and early-spring baby races, and "maiden special weights" for two-year-olds commonly first appeared in condition books in mid-May or even later.

Affirmed and Alydar both had reason, based on their heritage, to come to hand early as two-year-olds. Each would do so under the care of trainers from different generations and backgrounds, but both born to horse racing.

Lazaro Sosa Barrera, Laz to family and friends, which included almost everyone acquainted with him, was a native of Havana, Cuba, born near that city's legendary Oriental Park racetrack fifty-three years before Affirmed reached the races.

One of twelve children (nine boys), Barrera grew up around the races. In 1945 he immigrated to Mexico, where he began a successful training tenure that ended when he decided to try his hand in Southern California in 1960.

His stable in Mexico included seventy horses; his first in California was a one-horse operation for which Barrera did everything but ride. His break came when veteran trainer Bill Winfrey (of Native Dancer fame) hired him to take over his horses while Winfrey took some time off.

That exposure brought a few owners his way, and he gradually built a solid clientele and a good reputation as an astute judge of horses and their proper placement. His first stakes win came with Manassa Mauler in the 1961 Queens County Handicap in New York and that, too, brought him to the attention of additional owners, especially Latin Americans who raced in Florida, California, and New York.

Barrera enjoyed success with a variety of horses, including a number of stakes performers such as Acorn and Mother Goose stakes winner Windy's Daughter, the talented California-bred gelding Royal Owl, Princely Native, Raisela, Katonka, Due Diligence, and 1976 three-year-old standout Life's Hope, both of the latter owned by Harbor View Farm.

In fact, 1976 would be the year that Barrera "arrived" as a national figure in the racing game, but it was not Life's Hope or Due Diligence who would fuel his ascendancy.

Instead, Barrera's platform was the sturdy back (and legs) of an American-bred, Puerto Rican-owned colt named Bold Forbes, whom the trainer picked up, a bit reluctantly, after the two-year-old son of Irish Castle (a Bold Ruler horse) destroyed the fields in five straight races in Puerto Rico. His owner, Esteban Rodriguez Tizol, wanted to send him to New York, but his local trainer fell ill and could not go, so Barrera was asked to take a look.

What he saw was a compact, smallish youngster with warm shins, suggesting leg problems ahead. Barrera wasn't keen on using stall space for such an uncertain prospect, but was cajoled by the owner into doing so, then had to battle to get an extra stall for him.

Bold Forbes, ouchy shins and all, made his customary wire-to-wire effort in the Tremont Stakes at Belmont Park and the Saratoga Special, winning both by serious daylight in fast times.

The shins, and a later virus, stopped him at that point, and Barrera sent him to California for the winter. Santa Anita did not seem to suit the colt for a long while (he lost three in a row, albeit running competitive races), until Barrera cut holes on the side of his blinkers so he could see horses alongside him, and he won the one-mile San Jacinto Stakes.

Back in New York, Bold Forbes blistered Aqueduct's main track in the Bay Shore Stakes, running seven furlongs in 1:20 4/5, then really stepped up with a stakes-record 1:47 2/5 for one and one-eighth miles in the Wood Memorial, an impressive win that made him a serious Triple Crown candidate.

Barrera, knowing his horse could go a half in :45 right out of his stall, had concentrated on long, strong gallops with Bold Forbes, trying to get him distance-fit and more relaxed.

Kentucky Derby Day was May 1, 1976, and Bold Forbes made the 102nd Derby his own show. He jumped out of the gate on top, surged to a five-length lead heading down the backstretch, and then turned back a persistent bid by odds-on favorite Honest Pleasure to win by a length.

His fractions were quick: :22 2/5 for a quarter; :45 4/5 for a half-mile; six furlongs in 1:10 2/5; a mile

in 1:35 3/5. Horses usually stop in the Derby after setting such fractions, but Bold Forbes had legs of steel and
the heart of a lion. His final clocking of 2:01 3/5 was
extraordinary for a horse who only weeks before was
still being labeled a sprinter.

After Bold Forbes and Honest Pleasure cooked each
other in a speed duel in the Preakness (Bold Forbes
was third), Barrera's patient routine of long gallops
paid off again when the doughty little colt went wire to
wire to win the one and a half-mile Belmont Stakes, a
wonderful tribute to the horse, the trainer, and jockey
Angel Cordero.

This masterwork would earn Barrera and Bold
Forbes Eclipse Awards, Barrera as Trainer of the Year
and Bold Forbes as three-year-old champion, and
would certify Barrera's place among the top horsemen
in America. For most trainers, a horse like Bold Forbes
never arrives; if one does, it usually sets the seal on a
career. For Laz Barrera, the joy ride was just beginning.
There truly was "a better one in the barn."

For thirty-year-old John Veitch, being hired by
Calumet Farm in mid-April of 1976 was a fairy-tale-
come-true.

"I was in Florida with seven or eight bad horses and one good allowance horse when I was approached by Calumet's farm manager, Melvin Cinnamon, who said the Markeys were thinking of making a change," said Veitch. (Reggie Cornell had been training the Calumet horses since the late sixties.)

After more conversation, Cinnamon told Veitch the Markeys wanted to have lunch with him at their winter home in Miami. "I went thinking this was an interview, but soon realized they had already decided to hire me," said Veitch.

A bit mesmerized by this sudden change of fortune, Veitch took over a string of about twenty horses, including a two-year-old filly named Our Mims, who, as it turned out, was about the only racehorse in the bunch. Veitch had his father, Hall of Fame trainer Syl Veitch, to turn to for advice, but not much helped that first year.

The young trainer struggled, and the only light at the end of the tunnel was a nice-looking group of young horses at the farm. "Beginning around the first of October, I would go down a couple of times a month to visit with Melvin and Ewell Rice (the long-time

Calumet employee who broke the yearlings)," said Veitch. Among the twenty or so yearlings he saw were youngsters by Herbager, Raise a Native, Nashua, and the farm stallions.

"Mrs. Markey was appalled by what she regarded as 'exorbitant' stud fees, and tended to patronize the outside sires the farm had already had success with," said Veitch.

Rice and Cinnamon were really impressed with Sweet Tooth's strapping chestnut son by Raise a Native, named Alydar, but Veitch wasn't sure he would get to train him.

Alydar's name was a matter of some speculation, with conventional wisdom being that Lucille Markey named the colt after her great friend Prince Aly Khan, whom she often called "Aly, darling." Admiral Markey would call Veitch one day to tell him that this wasn't true, that the horse was named for a character in one of the Admiral's novels. Veitch, not having read those novels and being sensitive to the moment, would let the matter rest.

Veitch's problem, as he imagined it, was that Calumet runners earned only $87,725 in 1976, the farm's worst showing since the Great Depression, and Veitch thought he might soon be in a bread line.

"I thought I might be asked to resign when we met in the fall, and I apologized profusely, preparing to go graciously, but Mrs. Markey said it wasn't my fault, that 'we gave you some bad horses. Melvin says the two-year-olds and yearlings look pretty good.'"

Veitch breathed a sigh of relief and prepared to take his stable to Hialeah in December. Alydar would join them, but with fired shins.

"He developed bumps on his shins in November, and we decided to fire them as a precaution. Raise a Native's reputation for getting horses with leg problems influenced the thinking," said Veitch.

The shin firing routine, whether needed or not, was of no consequence to Alydar as he started his early racing lessons. "From the time we started him off at Hialeah, he was the star of the class," said Veitch. "He took everything in stride, nothing bothered him. His only problem was a tendency toward colic. If anything excited him when he ate, you set your watch on him showing signs fifteen or twenty minutes later."

Once they had that problem figured out, Veitch and

his crew led a charmed existence with the colt, who Veitch said "really showed a lot of promise, a lot of ability in the spring as a two-year-old."

He also showed a lot of speed, drilling five furlongs in :58 2/5 one morning under jockey Jorge Velasquez, meaning any maiden race with his name in the entries might be hard to fill.

Nevertheless, Veitch had him entered in one in early June, but the track came up muddy for his workout the day before, and Veitch opted instead to do the unusual and run him in a stakes race, the Youthful at Belmont Park, on June 15.

Veitch's thinking was logical enough: early two-year-old stakes fields usually are populated by maiden winners that have started once or twice.

The field for the Youthful was typical. There were thirteen entered, eleven of which started. Nine of the eleven had won their previous starts, although only two of them in New York. One of those two was a colt named Affirmed, who had made his career bow on May 24 in a five and a half-furlong maiden special weight against nine other horses, five of them first-time starters.

Despite the Harbor View and Barrera connections, Affirmed went off at 14.30-1, making him the fourth longest price in the maiden race. Under apprentice rider Bernie Gonzalez, he broke on the lead and added steadily to his advantage, winning by four and a half lengths. His time of 1:06 was pedestrian, but he looked good enough to assure that his odds next time would be much less generous.

In the Youthful, Affirmed was second choice to, surprisingly, Alydar, the only first-time starter in the field. His workouts, pedigree, and the Calumet name helped make him 9-5 favorite.

Affirmed, with Angel Cordero Jr. aboard, broke alertly again, stayed on the inside in second place behind leader Buck Mountain, and then went to the lead in mid-stretch.

Alydar, meanwhile, broke slowly and was trapped behind horses coming out of the turn. He then staged a nice rally that didn't threaten the contenders. Cordero steered Affirmed to the front at the eighth pole, then rode him out to hold off 45-1 shot Wood Native. Alydar was fifth, beaten just under five lengths.

For the Calumet colt, whose inexperience had

shown, redemption would come soon. Nine days later, on June 24, he faced nine other maidens in a maiden special weight at five and a half furlongs. Favored again, Alydar and jockey Eddie Maple, who rode regularly for Veitch, got it right this time.

Breaking evenly, Alydar surged to the lead midway on the turn, then drew away to win by six and three-quarters lengths in a sparkling 1:04 1/5. Behind him, in order, were five first-timers, including Believe It (second), Sauce Boat (third), and Junction (fourth). All were stakes horses in the making.

It was now time for the first Affirmed-Alydar rematch, this one coming in the Great American Stakes on July 6, 1977. Despite the Youthful results, New York horseplayers were all over Alydar, betting him down to 4-5, while Affirmed was actually third choice at 4.60-1, behind Kentucky invader Going Investor.

The race was a two-horse affair that was over by the time they turned for home. Affirmed raced quickly to the lead, setting good fractions (:22 2/5, :45 4/5), with Alydar parked outside about two and a half lengths back in fourth. Getting a five-pound weight break (117 to 122), Alydar surged by Affirmed heading into the stretch and drew away to a three and a half-length win in 1:03 3/5 for the five and a half furlongs, only three-fifths of a second off the track record.

Alydar was now the talk of the racing world. Calumet was back, with Our Mims leading the three-year-old filly parade and her big, bustling two-year-old half brother looking like the Calumet stars of old. Comparisons to Citation as a juvenile were already surfacing.

The Tremont Stakes at Belmont on July 27 simply threw gasoline on the fire. Alydar, favored at 2-5, was facing Believe It again, along with the quick Jet Diplomacy. Believe It, an In Reality colt bred and owned by Hickory Tree Stable and trained by the redoubtable Woody Stephens, was thought by many local horsemen to be a good work in progress.

Believe It ran well in the six-furlong Tremont, tracking Jet Diplomacy and then heading that colt near the eighth pole, only to have the red menace from Calumet cruise by. Alydar won by one and a quarter lengths in 1:10, with Believe It a clear second and Jet Diplomacy third.

Barrera had decided after the Great American to

ship Affirmed west, looking for bigger bucks and perhaps an easier spot in the Hollywood Juvenile Championship at Hollywood Park. The race split into two divisions, and Affirmed drew into the first half, where he was 2-5 favorite, with jockey Laffit Pincay Jr. aboard.

Affirmed did what 2-5 horses are supposed to do. He took the lead at the break, putting away his only nominal competitor while whistling through a :21 3/5 quarter and :44 2/5 half, then coming home alone by seven long lengths in 1:09 1/5 for six furlongs, with the other seven starters running their own race.

Barrera was pleased by the race and what he saw as a more relaxed, mature Affirmed, whom he shipped back to New York, where the Saratoga meet was underway. Affirmed was being prepared for the Sanford Stakes on August 17 as a prelude to the Hopeful, in which Alydar would likely be a presence as well.

The Sanford, always best known as the race in which the mighty Man o' War had his colors lowered for the only time, would become notable in 1977 as the first public appearance of what would ultimately be a history-making partnership, that of Affirmed and young riding superstar Steve Cauthen. Pincay had a commitment at Del Mar and Barrera already was using Cauthen regularly.

Cauthen, a native of northern Kentucky, had burst on the scene rather startlingly in May of 1976, at age sixteen — although he'd practiced at being a jockey for years — riding first at River Downs in Ohio, then in Illinois, next at Churchill Downs, then finally in New York late in the year. He won 240 races in 1976, winning with more than twenty percent of his horses and riding earners of $1.24 million in purses. In 1977 he was handed two Eclipse Awards, one as the country's top apprentice and the other as the nation's outstanding jockey, and was everyone's favorite nephew.

Nicknamed, rather unimaginatively, "the Kid," Cauthen looked like a twelve-year-old and rode with the patience, judgment, and poise of a Hall of Famer. His second year would go even better, as he rode top horses coast to coast, winning relentlessly and remaining the same level-headed, self-effacing teenager we like young heroes to be.

In a year when Seattle Slew became the first horse ever to complete the Triple Crown while still unbeaten for his career and Forego was once again a weight-carrying marvel, Cauthen was named Sportsman of the Year by *Sports Illustrated*, the first racing personality so honored. About the only thing he hadn't done on his magical carpet ride was win a Triple Crown race. Perhaps in Affirmed he had a horse to take him there, too.

Affirmed and Cauthen, sporting Harbor View's familiar pink-and-black silks, would make short work of the Sanford's five other starters, allowing Jet Diplomacy and Tilt Up a chance to have their respective moments in the sun, then zipping by them in mid-stretch to draw away to a two and three-quarters-length win in 1:09 3/5 for six furlongs. Oddly, Affirmed's Hollywood win wasn't impressive enough for Saratoga bettors, who made him co-favorite with the fast Tilt Up.

Alydar skipped the Saratoga juvenile races, going instead to Monmouth Park to entertain New Jersey fans in the Sapling, in which he would face only four others, one of them the talented Regal and Royal, a local stakes winner. Alydar was 3-5 in the Sapling and went about his business properly, relaxing early behind leaders Noon Time Spender and Pipe Major, then sailing by on the outside to win by two and a half lengths, the six furlongs in 1:10 3/5.

Also notable was that he dealt with, and handled, a sloppy track for the first time.

The Hopeful Stakes is Saratoga's most prestigious two-year-old race and has often produced winners who go onto bigger things. The 1977 version seemed likely to do so, with Alydar, Affirmed, Tilt Up, Regal and Royal, and Saratoga Special winner Darby Creek Road completing a high-end, if small, line-up.

Alydar was even-money, Affirmed was 2.30-1, the weights were level (122 pounds), so there would be no excuses.

Tilt Up took the track early, with Darby Creek Road in attendance, followed by Affirmed, with Alydar two lengths behind his rival as they ran toward the turn through a :22 4/5 quarter. The pace heated up on the turn as Cauthen sent Affirmed after Tilt Up, and Maple, taking Alydar around horses, kept Affirmed in his sights.

Although Tilt Up appeared to be in the hunt at the head of the stretch, he really wasn't, for the big two were soon driving away from him and the others in a match race of their own. Affirmed had a head margin at the eighth pole, with Alydar driving hard on the outside, but Affirmed was unswerving, holding a straight and true course (he had drifted out in the Sanford) and edging away from Alydar to win by a half-length in a stakes record 1:15 2/5 for six and a half furlongs.

The win would tie Barrera for the Saratoga trainer's title, and it would also have special meaning for the Barrera family, since brother Willy broke and galloped Affirmed, and brother Luis trained him for Laz in New York before Laz settled in at Belmont for the summer.

Patrice Wolfson enjoyed a nostalgic moment of her own, visiting the winner's circle where the Jacobs family's Hail to Reason, trained by her father, had won the Hopeful on his way to two-year-old championship honors and a wonderful stud career.

Could it get better than this?

Amazingly, yes.

September 10 witnessed the eighty-eighth renewal of the Futurity Stakes, once America's most valuable and important two-year-old race, still significant but now not as meaningful as the Champagne in mid-October.

There was some indecision in both camps about running in the Futurity so soon after their ding-dong struggle in the Hopeful, but when George Cassidy stood in the starter's stand before the Futurity, Affirmed and Alydar were looking at him.

Rough Sea took the early lead on sufferance from Affirmed, with Alydar about two lengths back in third, through an opening quarter in :23 3/5, the half in :46 3/5. At that point, Affirmed had seen enough of Rough Sea and went on with matters, but Alydar was after him quickly, sliding off the rail and going up alongside his nemesis.

They ran the third quarter in :23 1/5 and entered the final furlong locked in nose-to-nose combat. Alydar gained a slight lead, and then Affirmed came back as the two ran so closely together that their riders had to use their whips on the side away from the other horse.

Affirmed literally inched his way back ahead as these two warriors plunged forward, then Alydar made one final lunge. It was a desperate photo for the win, with Affirmed getting the call by a nose. The final time: a superb 1:21 3/5 for seven furlongs on a less-than-glib surface.

Whew.

Turf historians were combing the records, trying to find a rivalry comparable among past two-year-old stars. For most, nothing like this had happened since Twenty Grand and Equipoise went at it in 1930, and there was more to come, with the Champagne Stakes on October 15 listed on both horses' dance card.

Barrera was in a groove with Affirmed and had no intention of fixing something that wasn't broken. Veitch, on the other hand, thought a change was in order with Alydar. He would replace Maple with Jorge Velasquez.

"Maple was a good rider, but I thought Jorge was maybe a little stronger, more aggressive. Alydar was a classic one-run horse, and it was a strong run, but I had concluded that to beat Affirmed we needed to make one strong rush at him," said Veitch.

He also added blinkers to Alydar's equipment, believing that might help him focus better early in the race, get his head into it earlier.

The fall weather in New York in 1977 was drearier than usual. Jockey Club Gold Cup Day, with the Champagne as a sub-feature, opened cloudy and damp, leaving the track sloppy, although the sun made an appearance in mid-afternoon.

Our two heroes, though, were in full blossom as they paraded postward along with four others in the race that might settle the 1977 two-year-old male championship.

Sauce Boat and Quadratic, as expected, went for the early lead, with Affirmed watching and waiting, and Alydar just behind him to the outside.

On the final turn, Affirmed eased between the pace-setters and Cauthen straightened him away in the stretch with a half-length lead.

Alydar, having taken the overland route, was in full flight by then. He rolled past Sauce Boat and Quadratic and took dead aim on Affirmed. The latter wasn't stopping, but Alydar, racing well away from Affirmed, was the stronger of the pair as they reached the final one hundred yards.

He surged by Affirmed and went on to tally a one and a quarter-length victory, running the mile in 1:36 4/5 in the mud.

Cauthen said he didn't believe Affirmed was comfortable in the going, and Barrera thought his horse might not have seen Alydar soon enough to respond.

Regardless, Alydar had beaten Affirmed in the biggest juvenile event of the year, handily. Their score now read: Affirmed-three, Alydar-two, with Alydar winning his two by open daylight.

Veitch has always believed that the two-year-old male Eclipse Award would have been Alydar's had they stopped after the Champagne, and perhaps he is right.

Neither horse stopped, though, going on to Laurel Park in Maryland for the Laurel Futurity on October 29.

Barrera had said his horse wouldn't go if it rained and that this was his last start of the year, regardless. If he ran at Laurel he would head to the West Coast for rest and Triple Crown preparations.

If it rained, he would go to the Norfolk Stakes at the Oak Tree meeting at Santa Anita in November.

It didn't rain, and both horses showed up for what would surely decide the two-year-old title and leave one the early favorite for the 1978 Kentucky Derby.

The field facing them was debatable; in fact, for a while it looked as if there would be no field until multiple stakes winner Star de Naskra, locally owned, was supplemented for five thousand dollars, with a couple of claimers also then being entered.

Alydar, a slight underdog in the betting for the Futurity and Champagne, was 2-5 at Laurel, with Affirmed at 7-5.

Vince Bracciale Jr. bounced Star de Naskra out of the gate and into the lead, with Affirmed second, running well out from the rail, and Alydar lapped on him while racing on the inside.

Tactics were at work, for Barrera wanted Cauthen in a position where he could see Alydar at all times. The trainer did not want to risk having him slip up on Affirmed as he had in the Champagne.

Velasquez, down on the rail, would have to run Affirmed's race, which he did, splitting Star de Naskra and Affirmed on the final turn in an effort to get by his archrival before the stretch run.

Alydar got the lead, but ever so narrowly, and Affirmed was right with him, this time the outside horse, as they steamed for home.

Affirmed gained a slight but decisive advantage in mid-stretch and held to the wire, winning by a neck, although Alydar was nibbling at that margin at the end. By the length of Affirmed's neck, a championship was won, and lost.

Barrera summed up the race, and the year, when he told a *Blood-Horse* correspondent afterward, "There is never a disgrace when one of them loses. This is the sixth time now that they have run against each other, and it is the sixth time they both have run their race."

Affirmed needed to do no more, and Barrera took his medium-sized (fifteen hands, three inches at that time), beautifully balanced Formula One racecar horse to California for the winter.

Veitch, smarting from the Laurel Futurity loss and frustrated by his decision to run there, found his horse tearing down the barn after the Laurel race and decided that one more trip to the well would be okay, an opportunity to end the season on a winning note.

"I was a moron," says Veitch. "I was just trying to recoup the Laurel Futurity loss. If I had been older, I wouldn't have done it."

Nonetheless, he went postward in the one and one-eighth-mile Remsen Stakes on November 26 at Aqueduct against Believe It, fresh from a win in the

Keystone Stakes at Keystone Park in Philadelphia, and three others, including Quadratic.

Believe It was a colt of genuine merit, and he could be dangerous if he got loose on the lead over a sloppy surface like the one that ensued for the Remsen.

He did get loose and he was dangerous. He settled in front to set good but modest fractions, and then bounded away in early stretch to an insurmountable lead.

Alydar was well behind early, closed resolutely, but was still two lengths back at the finish as Believe It got the win in the excellent time of 1:47 4/5. Veitch had not put stickers (mud caulks) on his horse and thought that might have made a difference.

He was upset with his decision but headed off to Florida secure in the knowledge that his horse was "tremendously sound — an iron horse" and that the distances of the races in front of them in 1978 would be friendly to Alydar, maybe more so than to Affirmed, hopefully, possibly.

Affirmed, with a four-to-two advantage over Alydar, swept year-end honors and headed the Experimental Free Handicap at 126 pounds, with Alydar at 125 and Believe It at 124.

Racing fans across America had something to debate over the winter, a classic East-West rivalry between two superior talents.

No one, though, could anticipate what the future held.

CHAPTER 4

Perfect Preps

T he seventies might have been the best decade ever in American racing, bearing witness to more racecourse greatness than any ten-year span deserved.

Secretariat, Seattle Slew, and Affirmed would win Triple Crowns, and Spectacular Bid and Forego would race themselves onto near-equal footing with that trio. Ruffian would leave behind indelible impressions, and Canonero II, Riva Ridge, Key to the Mint, Foolish Pleasure, Bold Forbes, and dozens more champions and would-be champions would make the seventies roll call of brilliance longer and more memory-laden than those of any other comparable period in American racing history.

The seventies was also kind to the venerable Experimental Free Handicap, the contrivance begun in 1933 by racing Renaissance man Walter Vosburgh to place a theoretical weighting on the year's best juveniles.

As a predictor of future classic form, the Experimental had its good and bad sequences. After a good run in the 1940s with six classic winners from twelve highweights, the Experimental had a rough patch for the next two decades, with only one classic winner (Native Dancer) among the fifties' highweights and none in the sixties.

By the end of the seventies, six top-weighted colts would win classics, including the three Triple Crown winners, and two of the other four highweights would place in classics.

Some observers felt that both Affirmed and Alydar merited higher weights than the respective 126 and 125 pounds they were assigned by Experimental compiler and New York Racing Association racing secretary Tommy Trotter, a prudent, even cautious evaluator of Thoroughbreds.

As matters turned out, Trotter got the spread between the two about right, but he got the weights themselves too low, way too low.

When our two protagonists parted company in the fall at Laurel, Affirmed headed for Santa Anita and Alydar, after his unfortunate side junket to New York for the Remsen, to Hialeah Park. The latter, although steadily losing its luster as the centerpiece of Florida racing, was still home to one of the country's best racing surfaces, a main track that was both fast and deep.

Veitch recalls that after giving the Raise a Native colt a couple of weeks of relaxed exercise, he started asking Alydar for more effort and "everything went perfectly for him in Florida. We never had to miss any time because of weather."

Barrera, on the other hand, while he seemed to take matters in stride, could not have been thrilled with the turn of events, weather-wise, in California. As happens sometimes during a Los Angeles winter, the rains came to visit in early January and decided to take up semi-permanent residence at least through February.

Affirmed spent a lot of time walking the shed row during those months, getting long gallops and sporadic works when the weather permitted. One thing unimpeded, however, was his physical improvement. Measured at fifteen hands, three inches in late fall of his two-year-old season, he clearly grew in height and depth over the next few months, leaving behind the lean, almost effeminate look of his juvenile days for a stronger, if still sleek, visage.

Enjoying a much drier Florida winter, Alydar moved smartly ahead in his training regimen and stripped fit and fiery for his sophomore debut in a seven-furlong allowance test at Hialeah on February 11. Giving weight to all but one of his seven opponents, he ran like a 3-10 choice should, toying with his field as he cruised home by two lengths that could have been ten in 1:22 1/5, galloping out a mile in 1:35 3/5.

Veitch wasn't sure the seven-furlong race "would make him do enough" to be fit for the Flamingo Stakes on March 4, a one and one-eighth-mile test that was then the most important winter trial of a Triple Crown wannabe in the East.

The horse who had upset him in the Remsen, Believe It, was also at Hialeah, and trainer Woody Stephens had him looking good for the Flamingo off a seven-furlong score in the same time as Alydar's.

Alydar worked a mile in 1:37 2/5 on the Monday before the Flamingo; then Veitch continued his pattern of giving him a short, sharp work the day before the race.

"You had to train him, give him a lot of work, or else he would be dull," says Veitch. "I once worked him twice in one morning; sent him three-eighths in

:37 4/5, and he didn't do enough. I sent him back to do a quarter in :23 or so."

Veitch, feeling that Believe It was only a serious threat if the colt got an easy lead, entered another Calumet three-year-old, Hugable Tom, to make sure Believe It had a friend with him on the front end, if necessary.

It wasn't.

Longshot Slap Jack took Hugable Tom, Junction, and Believe It through fast early fractions (:23 3/5, :45 3/5, 1:09 4/5), before Believe It strolled by at the three-eighths pole with Alydar shadowing him on the outside.

Those two were a team turning into the stretch, but Velasquez asked Alydar for his best and drew away steadily and easily, finishing four and a half lengths in front of second-place Noon Time Spender, with Believe It dropping back to fourth. Alydar's final time was 1:47, only a fifth of a second off Honest Pleasure's stakes record and a clear indication that the East Coast king of the three-year-old hill was better than ever.

Four days later Affirmed made his first start at Santa Anita and any doubts about his readiness were over after a half-mile when he stormed to the lead, dusting his allowance rivals by five lengths and more, running six and a half furlongs in 1:15 3/5 as a 1-5 favorite.

As the rains would not relent, Barrera toyed with the notion of sending Affirmed to Louisville by the New York route, as he had Bold Forbes, but decided to stick it out at Santa Anita after the colt's allowance pipe-opener.

Next up was the San Felipe Stakes on March 18, but the question of the day was whether Affirmed and Cauthen would go to work as a team. The young jockey had a difference of opinion with the Santa Anita stewards over a ride and drew a suspension for his misjudgment. Knowing the suspension would cost him the San Felipe check, he went to court to get a stay of the suspension.

The court obliged, and Cauthen was aboard the Harbor View star when the gate latch was sprung for the San Felipe. It probably wouldn't have mattered if Cauthen's mother had ridden Affirmed because he quickly took care of business, racing just off the lead until he felt obliged to win his race, then running off to a two-length win in 1:42 3/5 for one and one-sixteenth miles.

He hadn't met a horse of Believe It's caliber, but Affirmed was acting very much like Triple Crown favorites are supposed to act.

Trouble was, so was Alydar. Tacked up for the Florida Derby at Gulfstream Park on April 1, he again faced Believe It, who had just lost to the unbeaten Majestic Prince colt Sensitive Prince in the Fountain of Youth Stakes.

Alydar, a leisurely gate horse, actually joined his six rivals in departing at the same time for once and was close to the leaders heading into the far turn, where he swept to the lead. Believe It, restrained early, went up to challenge and got alongside Alydar at the eighth pole, but Velasquez rapped Alydar twice and the pair surged ahead, winning by two lengths in 1:47.

Veitch liked what he was seeing thus far, believing his colt had visibly improved from two to three and possessed more acceleration and better focus. Meanwhile, he watched the California weather, and Affirmed's progress, with interest, thinking that perhaps the superior conditions in Florida might give Alydar a conditioning edge on his rival.

One day after the Florida Derby, Affirmed tried his wings on a cool, damp day in the Santa Anita Derby. Eleven three-year-olds decided to test him and his temporary companion, Laffit Pincay Jr., in the one and one-eighth-mile Derby. Pincay had won a coin toss with Angel Cordero Jr. for the mount as they vied to replace Cauthen, who was serving the aforementioned suspension, which had been upheld by California racing authorities.

Pincay's good fortune continued in the race when Affirmed gave him the proverbial rocking-chair ride. Second at the first call, Affirmed took the lead and completely dominated in the stretch drive, drawing away to an eight-length victory in 1:48.

With Alydar headed for Keeneland's Blue Grass Stakes on April 27, Barrera had to make a choice. He could ship to New York for the Wood Memorial then on to Kentucky or stay put to run in the Hollywood Derby at Hollywood Park on April 16 and ship only once. To the surprise of some, he chose the latter path, simply moving his tack box across town to Hollywood.

Affirmed had eight horses that wanted a piece of him in the Hollywood Derby, including some new shooters. One of them, an Arizona-bred named Radar Ahead, probably not aware of Affirmed's reputation, contested the early pace with the 3-10 favorite in rapid fractions (:22 2/5, :45, 1:09 2/5).

Affirmed edged ahead at that point and had a two-length lead turning for home. Cauthen smacked his mount twelve times in the stretch run, and he held a two-length margin over Think Snow at the finish, the time being 1:48 1/5 for the nine furlongs.

Barrera was steadfast in his confidence after the Hollywood Derby, although several commentators expressed reservations about Affirmed's new front-running style and his workmanlike effort at Hollywood against competition of uncertain quality.

Despite the similar race results for the two colts, popular sentiment was tipping ever so slightly toward Alydar, who was back at his old Kentucky home awaiting the Blue Grass.

That race would mark one of those occasions in sport when competition becomes secondary to the moment. The Markeys, both confined to wheelchairs and in failing health, were at the farm but unable to cope with an afternoon at the track.

Keeneland President Ted Bassett, with a marvelous gift for sentiment, had the Markeys' car driven to a spot on the far turn rail, and Jorge Velasquez slipped Alydar away from the post parade to stand by the rail, saying to Mrs. Markey, "Here's your baby, my lady."

It was an afternoon to savor, an occasion that the 22,000 in attendance would long remember, the day when nearly fifty years of Calumet memories were melded together for an elderly couple watching, for the final time, the last great horse they would share.

Alydar gave them, and the Keeneland crowd, what they wanted, blowing by the leaders on the final turn and pulling away powerfully to thunderous cheers in the stretch. His final margin was thirteen lengths, his time 1:47 3/5 for nine furlongs. A spectator or two wondered whether Velasquez might have been better served by easing up earlier.

The trophy was handed to Veitch, who then had it delivered to the Markeys, and Lucille Markey held it with one hand and clutched her husband's hand with the other as they drove away to nearby Calumet. There were few dry eyes at Keeneland, and many in attendance knew they had been part of a salute to history.

There was, however, a Kentucky Derby to be run nine days later, a race in which Calumet had a very live chance to win a record ninth trophy.

CHAPTER 5

Crowned

No one is entirely sure why the Kentucky Derby has become the most glamorous, sought after horse race on the planet. Tradition, location, and timing have something to do with it, as does intense, sometimes suffocating media coverage of the sort usually associated with season-ending championship events, which the Derby isn't.

It is an inexplicable phenomenon, but come the first Saturday each May, the racing world's eyes turn to Louisville, Kentucky, and horsemen who otherwise are about as un-Kentucky-like as possible choke up at the sound of "My Old Kentucky Home" and pray that they'll someday have a starter in the Derby.

A Derby winner? That goes beyond wishing and praying.

The 104th Derby was widely anticipated for the obvious

reason: the renewal of racing's best rivalry in years, possibly ever. As for the two principals, both appeared to be approaching their first meeting of 1978 in excellent order.

Affirmed worked one and one-eighth miles at Churchill Downs on Saturday, April 29, and traveled the trip in 1:56 1/5 on an off track. Barrera wasn't all that taken with his work initially, but decided, upon reflection, that it was a solid effort, especially his final half-mile. Affirmed went back to the track on Wednesday morning, and this time picked up his feet very quickly, zipping five furlongs in :59, signaling his sharpness and good spirits.

Alydar, coming off a Blue Grass that was more like a long, fast workout, went a half-mile in :50 on Tuesday, then did a :37 2/5 three-eighths in his customary Friday work. Veitch said later that he didn't like the way Alydar went in the half-mile work. "He didn't do anything wrong, but he gave me a cloud of doubt. I just don't think he extended himself over the Churchill strip."

There would be nine others lined up to face the Derby starter, including Believe It, coming off an impressive win in the Wood Memorial, and Sensitive Prince, unbeaten in six starts and trained by the masterful Allen Jerkens. Jerkens felt his colt had the talent, but possibly not the seasoning, to handle the Derby's pressures.

Affirmed drew post position two, Alydar ten, with the expected speed horses Raymond Earl in the number-one post and Sensitive Prince on the outside, which led Jerkens to hope he could be covered up behind other horses and rated.

Probably based on Calumet sentimentalism, the crowd of 128,000 made Alydar the 6-5 favorite, with Affirmed at 9-5, Sensitive Prince at 9-2, and Believe It at only 7.40-1.

The race went almost as one would have forecast, with one glaring exception. Raymond Earl dashed quickly to the front with Affirmed sitting comfortably behind him and Sensitive Prince chasing down the leader going by the stands the first time.

The latter, running aggressively, grabbed the lead on the first turn from Raymond Earl, with Affirmed bowling along comfortably in third, Believe It tracking him. Barrera had told Cauthen to sit behind the speed, if any developed, but cautioned him not to have a horse parked outside him, boxing him in and allowing Alydar to slip by.

But, where was Alydar?

Off satisfactorily, Alydar was slow into stride and had dropped seventeen lengths off Sensitive Prince's rapid pace (:22 3/5, :45 3/5) by mid-backstretch. Velasquez would say afterward that Alydar seemed uncomfortable with the track surface and that he was already working on him by the first turn. Working and getting no response.

Cauthen, on the other hand, was sitting as pretty as he could hope to be.

The game and gritty Believe It rushed up on the outside and slid by the fading Sensitive Prince on the final turn, taking a slight lead just before reaching the quarter pole.

Cauthen, though, was pushing Affirmed, letting him know the moment of truth was at hand, and, as always, there was a response. He nudged ahead of Believe It, increasing his margin to two lengths at the eighth pole. Finally, from out of the clouds, Alydar had chosen to make an appearance and was now rushing toward Affirmed, but with four lengths to make up in the final furlong.

He couldn't do it, but he at least made things respectable, finishing one and a half lengths behind

Affirmed in second, one and a quarter lengths ahead of third-place Believe It. The final time was 2:01 1/5.

The 104th Derby was now in the books. Affirmed had won it, demonstrating for the twelfth time in fourteen career starts his superior ability and temperament for racing. After a springtime of speculation, he had turned back his archenemy for the fifth time in seven meetings.

Possibly, Alydar had not run his optimum race, but Barrera was confident that his horse was unconquerable over any trip. Veitch was gracious in defeat, puzzled by Alydar's struggle with the Churchill ground, and prepared to head for Baltimore and round two.

Both horses shipped to Belmont prior to traveling to Pimlico for their eighth head-to-head encounter, but the next steps were considerably different, reflecting the respective mindsets of their trainers. Barrera, confident that his horse was physically at the top of his game and even more comfortable with Affirmed's tactical advantage, worked the colt only once between the Derby and Preakness. He sent him a mile in 1:40 1/5 at Belmont on May 13, a week before the Preakness.

Veitch, while he would make no equipment or other changes in Alydar's routine, had seen his pre-race worries about the burly colt's comfort with Churchill's surface apparently borne out in the Derby. Wanting no repetition in the Preakness, he shipped Alydar to Pimlico for a six-furlong work on the Monday before the race and watched him fly through six furlongs in 1:10 2/5 in the slop.

The colt's usual day-before work was a sharp three furlongs in :35. These moves suggested not only that Alydar could handle Pimlico with alacrity, but also that he was mentally focused.

Pimlico management, meantime, was scrambling to find horses willing — never mind able — to face the big two. Believe It, off a strong Derby effort, was back for another try, but that was it from Louisville. Four others were found, the best of them the consistent Noon Time Spender, a tough Florida-bred who had chased Alydar respectably, if not threateningly, during the winter. He would start at 80.80-1, the shortest price of the four back-enders.

Affirmed, having finally made believers out of horseplayers after the Derby, was favored at 1-2, with

Alydar at 9-5 and Believe It at almost 7-1. A good betting race it was not; as high drama, it would be almost as good as it gets.

The main question before the 103rd Preakness was one of pace; specifically, who would set it? Most writers and commentators thought Affirmed might end up in front by default, thereby creating a tactical dilemma for both Believe It and Alydar, particularly the latter.

However, longshot Track Reward, third in the Wood Memorial, trained in New York by Barrera's son Albert but owned by Marylanders, would settle that issue by breaking quickly and going to the lead, with Affirmed alongside and Believe It just behind.

Alydar had settled in toward the back of the field, but never more than six lengths off the lead, which became Affirmed's as they came out of the first turn. Cauthen, knowing the pace was moderate and that Track Reward was no speed maven, moved well enough ahead to ease over toward the rail, whereupon Cauthen throttled back, with Affirmed rating kindly through a half-mile in :47 3/5, six furlongs in 1:11 4/5.

At that point, most onlookers thought the race to be effectively over, with Affirmed in complete control, saving ground and strength. Even though Alydar had on his running shoes, the barriers to catching Affirmed seemed almost insurmountable.

Eddie Maple on Believe It and Herbert Hinojosa on Noon Time Spender, both recognizing that their best shot, given the pace, at testing Affirmed would come sooner than later, made almost simultaneous moves going into the final turn. They closed to the flanks of the Derby winner and his steady-as-she-goes pilot.

Cauthen, though, knew he had bullets left in the chamber and that these horses were not his targets.

He waited for the Calumet red and blue to show up in his field of vision, and when Cauthen and Affirmed approached the stretch Alydar was there, having steadily made up ground for three-eighths of a mile.

The crowd was in full-throated cry, for the awaited battle was now joined. Cauthen had the inside track and a fresh and supremely determined horse. Velasquez, whipping left-handed, nudged Alydar closer in early stretch, cutting the margin to a length, then a half, a neck, a head!

Each colt seemed to surge briefly; Affirmed edging away, Alydar reclaiming fiercely contested territory.

Believe It, always game, could not go with the two leaders this day, gradually falling away as the copper-coated gladiators continued their unyielding course to the finish.

Pimlico had seen its share of titanic stretch struggles before, but few more dramatic or more representative of the highest levels of Thoroughbred racing.

Yes, the real Alydar was back, in full battle gear. But he was battling the impenetrable defense of a horse who added indomitable will to the definition of competitor.

Affirmed, again, simply would not let Alydar go by. Velasquez did his best, and so did his equine companion in a superior display of power and tenacity. At the wire, Affirmed was in front by a neck, the time for the one and three-sixteenths-mile trip, 1:54 2/5, only two-fifths off the official race record. The winner had run the final mile of the race in a remarkable 1:36 1/5.

Woody Stephens, knowing Believe It's future lay wherever Affirmed wasn't, said: "That sucker — you've run into an iron wall when you get up to him."

Veitch and Velasquez, though disappointed, knew Alydar had brought his best stuff. Said Veitch, "I thought the Preakness would be better. We changed nothing tactically, and it was better, but not quite good enough."

Barrera had seen the race go as planned and could head to New York with the confidence of a man who knew he had an increasingly strong grip on the Triple Crown, perhaps an iron grip. Affirmed's victory also took him past the million-dollar mark in earnings, making him the youngest horse ever to reach that milestone.

Veitch, driving back to New York, decided that Alydar probably would be better off being positioned closer to Affirmed early. "But," said Veitch, "Alydar was a classic one-run horse, and you didn't want to make that run too early."

He believed that taking the blinkers off would give Velasquez the chance to send Alydar more readily as the tactical situation unfolded. "We wanted to take the fight to him sooner in New York," said Veitch. "I told Jorge, 'If Affirmed gets the lead and relaxes, stay close. As you turn down the backside, either be alongside him or where you can get to him.'"

Velasquez did all that he was asked to do in the Belmont, and Alydar did even more. His race was that of a Belmont winner, a Triple Crown winner, an all-time great.

As recounted earlier, no one can claim to have ever witnessed anything so wrenching and so grand as the last mile of the Belmont. As Veitch said, "It lived up to everybody's expectations."

Lou Wolfson, winner and loser of too many skirmishes to shed his poise, was reflective after his most meaningful triumph, acknowledging only that his horse was "a great three-year-old, and so is Alydar, but I want to see him run at four before I call him great overall."

One of horse racing's many old adages is that "the fittest horse wins the Kentucky Derby, the fastest horse wins the Preakness, and the best horse wins the Belmont."

This Belmont was center stage for two "best horses," either of whom would be worthy of the accolades reserved for the most storied winners of America's oldest and longest classic.

If Affirmed and Alydar had been given early retirement after that race, their names still would have been forever secured in racing lore.

One hundred and nine runnings of the Belmont had taken place, and a lot more would follow. Yet the 110th Belmont Stakes on June 10, 1978, is widely regarded as that great classic's finest hour.

CHAPTER 6

Rematch

Surely the strains of the Triple Crown, especially the muscle-challenging, lung-searing Belmont, would sap the strength of both Affirmed and Alydar.

Barrera, ecstatic after the Belmont, said his horse was in good shape, but would get a respite before returning to the wars at Saratoga, with the Travers Stakes on August 19 as his main objective. The trainer added Affirmed would likely race before then, perhaps in the Jim Dandy Stakes at Saratoga eleven days before the "Midsummer Derby."

Alydar, according to Veitch, came out of the Belmont in better shape than he had gone in. "He was physically and mentally stronger, more aggressive," said Veitch.

That led to a change in plans, since Veitch hadn't intended to run him before Saratoga, where his target would also be the Travers.

But no, here was Alydar, only six weeks after the grueling Belmont, visiting Chicago for the Arlington Classic, a race with a rich history that has Calumet written throughout. The farm had bred and owned five Classic winners prior to Alydar's race. He would face a nondescript group of four in what amounted to a ten-furlong exhibition for the big horse.

Alydar was 1-20 (show betting was not permitted), and he could have been 1-100 if the tote system had allowed. Ridden by Jeff Fell, who was subbing for the previously committed Velasquez, he galloped along in second place until the final turn. From there he went to the lead and drew away so easily that his final margin was thirteen lengths and his time 2:00 2/5.

Midwest tour behind him, Alydar was now pointed at Saratoga's prestigious Whitney Stakes on August 5, in which he would face more serious horses. Among them was the fleet J. O. Tobin, the first horse to beat Seattle Slew and fresh off a big win in the Tom Fool Handicap.

There were seven others, all stakes horses, on the track for the Whitney. Alydar was carrying 123 pounds and giving away actual weight to all except J. O. Tobin, who would haul 128, although on the scale of weights he would be getting two pounds from the Calumet star.

More than 31,000 fans, a record first-Saturday crowd for Saratoga, turned out to see what was expected to be a tough test for Alydar. He was made the 7-10 favorite by that crowd, and he put on what might have been his best performance in a distinguished career.

Rated in seventh place early, nine lengths off the three-year-old Buckaroo's fast pace (:23 3/5, :46 3/5, 1:10 2/5), Alydar and Velasquez had started to pick off horses one by one, moving up on the inside. Buckaroo, future sire of 1985 Kentucky Derby winner and Horse of the Year Spend a Buck, came slightly off the rail.

That opening gave Alydar room to ramble. He shot away from Buckaroo in a few strides, running off to a ten-length victory in 1:47 2/5, an eye-catching, invigorating performance and a real confidence builder for the Travers. Alydar could scarcely have been more impressive, thoroughly trouncing a quality field in fast time.

"When we got to Saratoga, I couldn't have been more confident," said Veitch. "Alydar was at the very top of his game. J. O. Tobin was a top horse, but Alydar couldn't have been better and was very convincing."

The Whitney was on Saturday; the Jim Dandy, on

Tuesday. Affirmed would face four opponents, only one of whom — Sensitive Prince — seemed to have any chance of troubling him.

The Jim Dandy is, of course, named for the winner of the 1930 Travers Stakes, in which the stakes namesake upset Triple Crown winner Gallant Fox on a wet track in dark, dreary conditions.

However, Sensitive Prince was trained by the upsetmeister himself, Allen Jerkens, noted for engineering monumental upsets with unheralded horses, including victories over such greats as Kelso and Secretariat. The horse was also rested, fit, and receiving nine pounds (128 to 119).

Similar to the 1930 Travers, the day was murky and wet, leading to a sloppy track and uneasy feelings among Affirmed's connections. Their ace was being asked to come back from an extended layoff and give nine pounds to a horse who would find the wet but fast conditions ideal for his front-running style.

Sensitive Prince would be most dangerous under such conditions, and he almost got his man, or horse. Jockey Jacinto Vasquez sent him to an immediate lead, and he put much daylight between himself and Affirmed, who seemed to be struggling to find his best stride.

The pace was good (:23 4/5, :46 3/5) but not outrageous, and the crowd began to wonder whether Sensitive Prince's lead — eight lengths after a half, four at the head of the stretch — would be too tough for a less than tightly wound Affirmed to overcome. Perhaps Cauthen would not persevere and would let the Jim Dandy serve as a belt-tightener for the Travers.

Here, however, was Affirmed stretching out, digging in, trying hard. He reduced the margin slowly and then more rapidly. Still, he seemed unlikely to get there even fifty yards out. A final driving thrust took him under the wire with Sensitive Prince, and his late burst was strong enough to earn him — truly earn him — a half-length win in 1:47 4/5, fine time on a sticky track.

It was, in its own way, an impressive win, but Alydar's victory was more so to many people, including his trainer.

"I watched Affirmed in the Jim Dandy," said Veitch, "and thought he was hard pressed, maybe weaker than in the Triple Crown races. Alydar was better than he'd ever been, and I was more confident for the Travers than any race we'd ever run against Affirmed."

Happy with his colt, Barrera was confident the Jim Dandy struggle would make him a fitter, better horse for the Travers. He did have one worry, though, however minor it might have seemed. Cauthen had injured his knee and shoulder in a spill the day after the Jim Dandy and had to take off a few days.

By Travers week, the few days of rest had been extended on the advice of his doctors, so he would not be aboard Affirmed in the Travers. As a precaution, Barrera had lined up Laffit Pincay, Affirmed's rider in the Santa Anita Derby, just in case. Problem solved.

The New York Racing Association had its own Travers problem, which was trying to ensure that the 109th running of the mile and a quarter event would be something more than a match race.

Finally, trainer Phil Johnson said he would run Brooklyn Handicap winner Nasty and Bold. The formerly Puerto Rico-based Shake Shake Shake was then entered late. Fifth in the Monmouth Invitational the day Alydar won the Whitney, he was to be piloted by Angel Cordero.

Saratoga was stuffed for Travers Day.

A record crowd of 50,122 attended, some going into

the infield, which was opened to patrons for the first time in memory. Media attention was overwhelming, with Triple Crown-like interest. The only horsemen not there were either dead or racing elsewhere.

By the 5:45 p.m. post-time, sweaty palms were much in evidence. As the gates opened, Affirmed was 7-10 and Alydar was even money.

Pincay went directly to the lead in the middle of the track, with Shake Shake Shake hustled up inside him by Cordero. Affirmed was setting easy fractions (:24, :48, 1:11 3/5), but Pincay was uncomfortable outside Shake Shake Shake, who drifted on the first turn and moved clear of him down the backstretch.

Velasquez, sensing the pace was not strenuous, steered Alydar down to the rail and moved up to the leaders just before they reached the final turn.

What happened next depends on whether you share the view of Laz Barrera, Laffit Pincay, Jorge Velasquez, John Veitch, or the stewards, whose views would ultimately be the only ones that mattered.

As Alydar moved up the fence, Shake Shake Shake dropped back, leaving Affirmed with about a half or three-quarters-length lead over Alydar. At that moment, Pincay moved his horse to the rail, making contact with Alydar's right front, causing the Calumet colt to pull up abruptly, barely missing contact with Affirmed's rump.

Alydar drifted to the middle of the track, almost in slow motion, and Veitch feared he had broken down. Surely, he would be pulled up, out of the race.

As if he knew this was important, Alydar rallied and on his own momentum set out after Affirmed. He rushed up to Affirmed's outside in early stretch, cutting the lead to two lengths, but understandably flattened out in the run to the wire, trailing the victorious Affirmed by one and three-quarters lengths.

The stewards immediately lit up the inquiry sign, and Velasquez claimed foul as soon as he arrived at the weigh-in scales. The race film told the story simply and profoundly. This was an easy, if unpleasant, call: Affirmed was disqualified and Alydar moved up.

No one celebrated, not Veitch nor Velasquez, who felt his horse was going to win on merit and was upset that Alydar's chances were compromised. Barrera was a raging bull after the race, yelling that Cordero had tried to get his horse beaten and that Velasquez had risked everybody's safety trying to go inside. He went as far as to say that Affirmed would never run against Alydar again.

Thus, the Travers, the tenth meeting of Affirmed and Alydar, had ended unsatisfactorily, none of the intriguing questions about the relative merits of these two great Thoroughbreds having been answered.

Veitch said he was "perhaps even more disappointed than after the Belmont. I was really upset with Pincay, who looked Jorge in the eye, then dropped over on him."

Tempers cooled, even if the debate didn't, and both horses were directed toward the Marlboro Cup. There they would meet Seattle Slew, 1977 Triple Crown winner but an uncertain quantity coming off a loss in the Paterson Handicap at the Meadowlands.

Slew's post-Triple Crown experience had been unsettling, with a bad loss in the Swaps Stakes (to J. O. Tobin), the eventual firing of trainer Billy Turner, a life-threatening virus in the winter of 1978, and a slow return to form amidst signs of bickering and confusion among his connections. At his best, Seattle Slew was a supreme front-runner, and his reputation was in need of quick repair, something that a win over Affirmed and Alydar would readily accomplish.

Yet Seattle Slew would not face the indestructible duo. After fifteen months and ten face-offs in races of the highest caliber, Affirmed and Alydar would be separated.

On September 11, five days before the Marlboro Cup, Alydar breezed a mile at Belmont and headed back to the barn in normal fashion. While walking the shed row, he showed signs of lameness in his left fore-leg, where X-rays revealed a fracture on the wing of the coffin bone.

The sesamoid on that leg had been banged up in his Travers mishap, but whether that and his subsequent injury were connected is unclear. In any event, he was confined to stall rest for eight weeks, his season ended.

His future? The veterinarians said he should recover well and that with reasonable luck he could return to the races at four. There was some discussion of retirement, but Mrs. Markey wanted to race him at four, so he stayed with the racing stable.

Affirmed was still very much on track for the Marlboro Cup, where he was assigned 124 pounds, conceding a pound by scale to Seattle Slew, who was carrying 128. Quality stakes winners Nasty and Bold, Upper Nile, Cox's Ridge, and Darby Creek Road filled out the dance card for this first-ever meeting between Triple Crown winners.

The 1978 Marlboro Cup, fittingly, would turn into a two-horse race between the highweights and would vindicate the long-held view that a high-class older horse, all things being equal, will always beat a high-class three-year-old.

Slew, a heavyweight with a Rocky Marciano-like body and the bone of a redwood tree, looked fit and fired up in the post parade. Angel Cordero was riding him for the first time. Cordero was replacing Jean Cruguet, who was fired after his comments about the horse's training.

After studying the field for the Marlboro, Barrera realized the only speed in the race other than Slew's was his own horse. He didn't really want to go head to head with a natural front-runner of Slew's undeniable ability, but he told Cauthen that he had to stay lapped on Slew unless the pace was torrid.

It was not.

Cordero, a master at grabbing the lead and slowing the pace, let Slew go to the front and amble through an opening quarter in :24, with Affirmed chasing but not close enough. Cauthen apparently was concerned about a suicidal speed duel and was confident in his horse's ability to run down any horse he could see, as Barrera had said — more than once — he would do.

After a half-mile in :47, Slew was ahead of Affirmed by two and a half lengths, which might as well have been five or ten. Seattle Slew, in peak form, was not going to be caught by any horse alive after a :47 half, and he soon showed the world what all the fuss the year before had been about.

There is nothing more awe inspiring in horse racing than a brilliant front-runner alone on the lead, and Slew had the look of eagles in the Marlboro.

With Affirmed now in full chase, Cordero asked his horse for his best gear, and Slew fired the retrorockets. After six furlongs in 1:10 1/5, he reached a mile in 1:33 3/5 and finished the mile and a furlong in 1:45 4/5, only two ticks off Secretariat's stakes, track, and world record. Throughout the stretch run, he maintained a three-length lead over Affirmed, whose own superior effort could not match a final five-eighths in :58 4/5.

The rest of the field? They watched in awe.

Wolfson and Barrera kicked around the possibility of running in the September 30 Woodward Stakes, in which they would again face the rejuvenated Slew. They elected to pass, deciding to train Affirmed for what would be his final race of the year, the mile and a half Jockey Club Gold Cup at scale weights on October 14 at Belmont.

Seattle Slew won the Woodward by four lengths. Those who thought he was best at nine or ten furlongs wondered whether he would even go in the mile and a half Gold Cup, but his connections confirmed his participation shortly after the Woodward.

Determined that Slew wouldn't waltz away with the Gold Cup without a battle, Barrera put in Harbor View's capable gelding Life's Hope as a pacemaker. Also in the field was the talented Exceller, an international star with top-class credentials on grass and dirt, and a horse sure to like the distance. Winner of eleven grade or group I races in three countries in a distinguished career, Exceller would be watching the pace from the back, his jockey, Bill Shoemaker, hoping for excessive speed.

He would get it, as Slew found both Affirmed and Life's Hope lapped on him after the gates opened.

The plan was for Affirmed to ease back after Life's Hope engaged Slew, but a slipping saddle under Cauthen left him with dubious control of his horse. Affirmed, to the chagrin of Cauthen and Barrera, was rank and uncontrollable, and the fractions the leaders were setting on a sloppy surface were astounding: :22 3/5, :45 1/5, 1:09 2/5, 1:35 2/5. Great numbers for going a mile or mile and one-eighth, unthinkable if the finish comes at the end of a mile and a half.

Slew was up by two and a half lengths over Affirmed after a mile, and at that point the three-year-old began to fall back. Slew went on valiantly, trying to hold off the charging Exceller. He almost did so, losing the lead and then coming back to miss by a heart-breaking nose. Affirmed, compromised by the loose saddle, ended up fifth, his only out-of-the-money finish ever.

Affirmed was finished for the year, having had a strange, disappointing late summer and fall, yet only in the Marlboro Cup was he legitimately beaten.

Before the Marlboro Cup in September, the New York Racing Association's chief examining veterinarian

Dr. Manny Gilman measured both Affirmed and Alydar. He found that Affirmed had grown considerably from two to three, standing 16.1 hands, to Alydar's 16.1 1/2, and measuring 74 1/2 inches at the girth, the same as Alydar. In fact, the two colts, perceived to be so different, were very much alike.

More important, while Affirmed clearly had the three-year-old male championship sewn up, drama surrounded the biggest of the Eclipse Awards, Horse of the Year. Seattle Slew, despite essentially disappearing after the Triple Crown, had beaten Forego for Horse of the Year honors in 1977. Would he repeat the feat in 1978 after besting that year's Triple Crown winner twice in the fall?

The voters, apparently feeling that Affirmed's full year of excellence, and the bad luck in the Travers and Jockey Club Gold Cup, offset Slew's terrific fall. They made Affirmed Horse of the Year and added Barrera's third straight Eclipse as top trainer and Harbor View as leading owner and breeder.

The Harbor View colt, none the worse for his fall misadventures, was headed west for a winter campaign at Santa Anita, beginning with the Strub series in

January and February, and the Santa Anita Handicap in March.

Alydar, still stall-bound, would head south to Hialeah Park in Miami with his stablemates. His fans waited and hoped he could return.

CHAPTER 7

Top Of His Class

Out of the eight Triple Crown winners since the year-end championship polls officially began in 1936, all were named Horse of the Year at the end of their three-year-old season.

Affirmed was one of that number, but a cloud of doubt covered his departure to winter quarters. More than a few observers questioned his rightful claim to the Horse of the Year mantle.

As often happens when championships are determined at the ballot box, the criteria for making such determinations are in the eye of the beholder. In years when there is no standout, voters gravitate to the horse or horses that end their seasons on a positive note. A win in a Breeders' Cup race, since the event's advent in 1984, has resulted in a year-end championship about fifty percent of the time. Breeders' Cup losers have accounted for another twenty-five percent or so of Eclipse Awards.

Prior to the Breeders' Cup, the closest surrogates were the major fall stakes races in New York. A horse winning one of those races in early fall was almost instantaneously elevated to championship contender status.

During the late seventies a three-year-old or older horse that won the Woodward, Marlboro Cup, and/or Jockey Club Gold Cup was typically on everyone's year-end championship short list, particularly if the horse won more than one of the three. In that scenario, Horse of the Year honors would also be looming.

For Affirmed's camp, the fall of 1978 was an unsettling time.

Their colt was on a nine-race roll heading into the Travers, which he subsequently won until the stewards took him down.

Following the Travers, Affirmed was officially at the top of his class. Unofficially, though, to a number of onlookers the Travers result suggested that Affirmed was vulnerable, that he might have peaked during the Triple Crown and was no longer at the top of his game.

Horse of the Year voters are sometimes required to

compare season-long consistency against belated brilliance. This raises the question, what is the Horse of the Year supposed to be, anyway? Is he or she the nation's best horse or its most consistent at the highest levels of the sport?

Affirmed's consistency was undeniable. Prior to the Travers, he had not lost since the Champagne Stakes the previous October. All but one of his nine subsequent successes were in major stakes races, and he had beaten the best of his generation so regularly, even Alydar, that he was solidly the leader of the three-year-old division.

And the Travers? Well, the race might have ended differently had Pincay not sealed Alydar off at the end of the backstretch. Alydar might have been ready to explode by Affirmed before the latter could adequately respond. Perhaps Veitch's pre-race confidence in Alydar was justified and his colt was, at that point, in better form. Alydar's recovery from the incident was remarkable, and he easily made up more ground than the distance by which he lost.

On the other hand, there was Woody Stephens' "iron wall" theory, which held that Affirmed was a

Affirmed and Alydar were "greatness on display, times two." The two valiant chestnuts gave horse racing some of its most thrilling moments.

Affirmed and Alydar shared the same sire line, that of Raise a Native. Affirmed was sired by Exclusive Native (top), a son of Raise a Native. Affirmed's female family was more workmanlike than spectacular. His dam, Won't Tell You (middle with a full sister to Affirmed), was a solid campaigner, as was her sire, Crafty Admiral (right), the 1952 champion handicapper.

Alydar was by Raise a Native (left), a precocious and speedy son of Native Dancer (above). Sweet Tooth (below left), the dam of Alydar, descends from one of Calumet Farm's storied brood-mares, Blue Delight. Alydar's broodmare sire, On-and-On (below), was a Calumet-bred out of champion Two Lea.

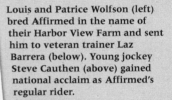

Louis and Patrice Wolfson (left) bred Affirmed in the name of their Harbor View Farm and sent him to veteran trainer Laz Barrera (below). Young jockey Steve Cauthen (above) gained national acclaim as Affirmed's regular rider.

Alydar recalled the glory days of Calumet Farm for Lucille Wright Markey (below), and catapulted trainer John Veitch (right with Alydar) and jockey Jorge Velasquez (above) to the sport's highest ranks.

Affirmed and Alydar's first meeting was inauspicious with Affirmed winning the Youthful (top) and Alydar finishing fifth. In their next encounter, the Great American (above), Alydar got the better of Affirmed, who later turned the tables in the Hopeful (left).

The colts' rivalry continued to build through the end of their two-year-old season: Affirmed edged Alydar in the Futurity (above); Alydar got the clear victory in the Champagne (right); and Affirmed held off his late-closing foe in the Laurel Futurity (below).

Affirmed and Alydar took different paths along the Derby trail. Alydar (above left with groom Clyde Sparks) wintered in Florida before coming to Kentucky where he demolished his Blue Grass rivals. Affirmed (left), who was named champion two-year-old colt, went to California, where he easily handled his competition in the Santa Anita Derby (below).

Affirmed and Steve Cauthen got to smell the
roses after a commanding victory in the
Kentucky Derby. Alydar closed late but not in
time to reach his rival.

Affirmed (on inside) and Alydar hooked up in the stretch of the Preakness and battled to the wire, with Affirmed prevailing by a neck. The Preakness set the stage for an even greater contest of strength and will — the Belmont.

Affirmed and Alydar's Belmont Stakes has gone down in racing history as one of the sport's greatest races. The two chestnuts were side by side with a mile to go in the mile and a half race. They dueled the rest of the way, neither giving an inch, until at the wire, Affirmed thrust his head in front to become racing's eleventh Triple Crown winner.

After the Triple Crown Affirmed waited until Saratoga to return, taking the Jim Dandy (left) in preparation for the Travers. Alydar came back earlier, winning the Arlington Classic and the Whitney (middle). The two met for what would be the final time in the Travers (bottom), but the result was dissatisfying. Affirmed won but was disqualified for interfering with Alydar, who was awarded the victory.

With new regular rider Laffit Pincay Jr., Affirmed became a dominant force at four, winning the Strub (top), Santa Anita Handicap, Californian (above), and Hollywood Gold Cup (below). Meanwhile, Alydar (below right) was attempting to come back from an injury suffered after the Travers.

After incurring another injury, Alydar was retired in July of 1979, while Affirmed continued to pile up victories. Affirmed captured the Woodward Stakes and received a congratulatory smooch from Barrera (below). Affirmed and Pincay (above left) headed to the track for the Jockey Club Gold Cup, in which Affirmed defeated Spectacular Bid and Coastal (above right). A few weeks later Affirmed was retired in a ceremony at Aqueduct (top right).

Affirmed sired consistent runners, many of which showed an affinity for the turf, a surface on which he never ran. Among his top offspring are European champion Zoman (top right), two-time champion Flawlessly (above), and Canadian Horse of the Year Peteski (right). Affirmed died in 2001 at age twenty-six and was buried at Jonabell Farm in Kentucky. A marker was to be placed on his gravesite.

Alydar often is considered the better sire while Affirmed gets the edge as a racehorse. Alydar, who stood at Calumet Farm during the farm's troubled years, died in 1990 at age fifteen under troubling circumstances. He had already made his mark as a sire, though. His outstanding progeny include the brilliant champion Easy Goer (top), Horse of the Year and Kentucky Derby winner Alysheba (top right), and champion filly Althea (above). Alydar is buried in the Calumet graveyard.

horse that just wouldn't let another get by him. Okay, put an asterisk by the Travers and move on to round two between the two rivals.

Just as it became hard to imagine that their rivalry could produce additional drama, Alydar's injury placed such matters, at least temporarily, on hold.

Affirmed had clear sailing to both the three-year-old and Horse of the Year awards. Or did he? The three-year-old championship might be in the bag, but challenges were looming on the older horse horizon, among them the prior year's Triple Crown winner Seattle Slew.

After the latter dusted Affirmed in the Marlboro Cup, won the Woodward, and outran a compromised Affirmed in his never-to-be-forgotten Gold Cup, the evidence on the matter of the best horse seemed settled. It was Seattle Slew, the four-year-old, albeit by only a pound or two.

The Eclipse voters, though, were slightly more enamored with Affirmed's long winning streak, Triple Crown sweep, and stirring victories over Alydar. This time, they apparently chose the tougher horse over the faster horse.

Barrera remained highly confident in his horse, feeling Affirmed had excuses in his last two starts, especially the Gold Cup. Others were not so sure, believing they had seen a horse who was tired and frayed in September and October. There were a few whispers that he was "cooked" and might not return to the races.

Even Wolfson's insistence that Affirmed was on track to a California-based four-year-old campaign would not still those voices, especially after the colt was syndicated into thirty-six shares, with Harbor View retaining fifteen, for a total of $14.4 million.

This was, of course, the stuff of the racetrack rumor mill, with no hint that Affirmed's connections were thinking of retiring him or believed his form was permanently compromised.

After all, here was a horse whose 1977 earnings ($901,541) were a single-season record. Here also was a horse who had won the most difficult of all racing prizes, the Triple Crown, in a gut-wrenching competition with a powerful competitor, and whose only legitimate loss was to one of the best front-runners in American racing history.

Affirmed would be back, and Barrera felt the four-year-old would prove himself to be among the best ever.

The trainer, frustrated by the Travers' outcome and Affirmed's subsequent races, was eager for a chance to silence the naysayers. Affirmed's fans, and those of Alydar, which collectively represented just about everyone in racing, were hopeful of further renewals of the best rivalry the sport had seen.

CHAPTER 8

Iron Wall

After a light training regimen for a few weeks following the Jockey Club Gold Cup, Barrera began stepping up the intensity of Affirmed's workouts in preparation for the first race in Santa Anita's Strub Series, the seven-furlong Malibu Stakes on January 7, 1979.

All being well, Affirmed would run in the mile and one-eighth San Fernando Stakes and the mile and a quarter Charles H. Strub Stakes, with the lucrative Santa Anita Handicap in early March his ultimate winter goal.

Affirmed was never noted as a "morning glory," and fast workouts were the exception, not the norm, so his five-furlong work in :58 3/5 on December 26 indicated he was on target for the Malibu.

The Strub Series is an anachronism of sorts, being restricted exclusively to four-year-olds. With the number of possible participants already limited, Affirmed's entry in the Malibu restrained enthusiasm for the race even further.

Four other horses lined up to face him, among them the talented Radar Ahead and the speedy Little Reb, who had won the six-furlong Palos Verdes Handicap on opening day at Santa Anita.

The weather earlier in the week had been wet, and more rain was forecasted for Malibu day, causing Barrera to say he might not run his horse. The day, in fact, was sunny and beautiful, but the track superintendent, expecting rain, had packed down the surface.

This left the track firm, but wet underneath, with the going on the rail somewhat slower than elsewhere. The track was rated as good at the beginning of the program and upgraded to fast later. But the rail was still suspect.

Affirmed, bet down to 3-10 (no show wagering) looked good, drawing sustained applause in the paddock before the race and appearing more muscular than he had been during his three-year-old campaign.

Breaking from the number two post position, Steve Cauthen soon found himself and Affirmed in a box behind the pace-setting Little Reb, with Radar Ahead sitting alongside.

Little Reb, getting six pounds from Affirmed and three from Radar Ahead, hummed along through a quarter in :22 2/5 and a half in :45, leading Radar Ahead by two lengths, with Affirmed another half-length behind. The champ was in striking distance, but when the moment came to go on, there was only a nominal response. Running on the rail all the way, Affirmed could only race evenly in the stretch as Little Reb edged away slightly to win by two and a quarter lengths with Radar Ahead in second, a head in front of Affirmed. The final time was 1:21, only two-fifths of a second off the track record.

The paddock cheers turned to scattered boos as Affirmed returned to be unsaddled. Cauthen told reporters he had no room to run at the three-eighths pole, then didn't have enough horse when he found space in early stretch.

Barrera was visibly upset with his jockey after the race, feeling that getting locked in on the rail was a significant tactical error in a sprint. Cauthen, though, probably had it right when he said that Affirmed would be tighter for his next trip, implying that chasing a good sprinter familiar with the track was not the way to strut Affirmed's stuff.

Nonetheless, the losing streak was now at four, and it was of no comfort that Affirmed would have come out as the best horse had all the entrants carried the same weight. While Little Reb and Radar Ahead were certified stakes competitors, neither should have been able to warm up Affirmed at his best.

The nine-furlong San Fernando, thirteen days later, figured to mean a lot more since Affirmed would have the benefit of a belt-tightener (the Malibu), additional training, and a two-turn race. These advantages figured to move him up.

The weights, under the allowance conditions of the Strub Series, would be the same, as would be the weather. A series of storms traveled through Southern California, dumping rain every couple of days. The track surface's varying stages of wetness made planning workouts and racing schedules quite difficult.

Affirmed, perhaps looking beatable to local trainers, would face seven horses in the San Fernando, including Little Reb, Radar Ahead, the good stakes winner Noble Bronze, and Elmendorf Farm's capable Syncopate.

The Santa Anita crowd, almost 40,000 for this race, still liked Affirmed's chances well enough to make him

1-2, with Radar Ahead at 4.20-1 and Little Reb at 6-1. The track was rated "good," but several observers thought it was slower than that. The rail was once again dead.

Cauthen made a point of staying off the rail from the outset in the San Fernando. When Affirmed dropped back to fifth heading onto the backstretch, his jockey reminded him that they were in a horse race. Little Reb had, as expected, grabbed the early lead and was in command down the backside and into the last turn, getting a quarter in :22 4/5, a half in :45 3/5, and six furlongs in 1:09 3/5.

Radar Ahead, under Darrel McHargue, was cruising along behind Little Reb in excellent striking position, and strike he did. With a quarter mile to go, he moved alongside the leader and edged ahead as they straightened for the stretch run.

Little Reb, though, was tenacious, hanging on with courage while Radar Ahead inched by. Meanwhile, Affirmed, in third place with a clear path to the leaders, was under pressure from Cauthen, who was getting only a modest response from his chestnut partner.

Radar Ahead finally broke Little Reb's last line of

resistance inside the sixteenth pole and started drawing away. Affirmed, lacking the old-time acceleration, gradually overhauled the exhausted Little Reb, beating the pacesetter by a neck. But Affirmed could make no dent in Radar Ahead's margin, finishing two and three-quarters lengths behind the leader, who completed the race in 1:48.

Barrera was less frustrated after the San Fernando than after the Malibu, saying his charge did not care for the track condition and "ran only in spots." Cauthen agreed, saying Affirmed was somewhat sluggish and "didn't seem to like the track at all."

If Affirmed had trouble getting a feel for the Santa Anita surface, Cauthen was having an even harder time. By the end of the day following the San Fernando, Cauthen had ridden eighty — yes, eighty — horses at Santa Anita without a single winner.

His losing streak would reach 110, by far the worst slump of his relatively brief career, and he would announce that he and agent Lenny Goodman were heading back to New York, at least for the time being.

Racing writers were fascinated by both Cauthen's horrendous winless streak and the mighty Affirmed's equally surprising fall from grace. They openly speculated that Affirmed had lost some of his competitive fire and might not find it for a while, if ever.

Barrera remained confident that his horse was as good as ever but was no longer so sure of Cauthen. Shortly after the San Fernando, Barrera announced a switch to Laffit Pincay Jr. for the Strub Stakes on February 4.

Cauthen changed his mind about leaving California and, instead, changed agents, hiring Harry Hacek in place of Goodman. Shortly afterward, the jockey would leave the United States to ride in England, where he could carry a bit more weight. He would compete for fourteen seasons in Europe, winning three British riding titles and two Epsom Derbys, and earning a reputation as a gentleman and a jockey of the highest caliber.

"The Kid," a master of the right move at the right time, was making what would turn out to be the best move of his career.

Affirmed, now working on his own five-race losing skein, was at least showing distinct signs of a return to top form, if workouts were any gauge. Barrera sent him five furlongs in :57 one morning. Then, in his last major effort before the Strub, the colt worked six furlongs in 1:10 3/5, galloping out a mile in 1:36 2/5.

These were not the workouts of a stale or tired horse, nor those of the old Affirmed — they were better. Affirmed looked good. He had thickened and added weight since his three-year-old season, and his coat and eye impressed all visitors.

The Strub Stakes, once called the Santa Anita Maturity, has a rich history as the ultimate jewel in the Strub Series and a key prep for the Santa Anita Handicap. At a mile and a quarter, it discourages the sprinters, and because of its allowance conditions, tests the pretenders. Weight spreads are reasonable, so the better horses aren't unduly penalized. The distance takes care of the rest.

Eight horses decided to come after Affirmed in the 1979 Strub, although only Radar Ahead would get any respect from the 50,220 fans in attendance, who made Affirmed 9-10 and Radar Ahead 3-2.

Longshot Quilligan Quail took the lead initially, with Johnny's Image in second as they moved through the opening quarter in :23, the half in :47, and six furlongs in 1:10 4/5.

The leaders were there only by Affirmed's indulgence, however, for on this day the Harbor View hero had his running shoes firmly laced. He broke alertly and was prominent early while racing well away from the rail, with Radar Ahead just behind him.

When asked by Pincay to get better position, he responded so forcefully that he swept quickly into the lead and then drew away powerfully over a track labeled "good," not dissimilar to the conditions he had faced previously in the Malibu and San Fernando.

The Strub was all his. The thunderous applause of the large crowd when he flashed under the wire ten lengths in front in the time of 2:01 indicated they knew they had seen a dominating performance by a horse who had clearly regained whatever he might have temporarily lost. This was a sharp, alert, and on-the-muscle Affirmed, ready and eager for all challenges.

Barrera talked to the press after the race about the jockey change, saying that part of his rationale was to take pressure off Cauthen. The trainer stated that Pincay would stay in the saddle while the colt raced in the West, but suggested that Cauthen might return when Affirmed headed east in the summer. Cauthen would, however, be in England long before that decision was due.

Pincay was thrilled to be back on his old friend, with whom he had never finished worse than first (the Travers disqualification being their only hiccup). He told reporters that Affirmed was so full of run that "I was only concerned with keeping him in the clear and out of trouble."

Next up was Santa Anita's pride and joy, the Santa Anita Handicap, known locally as the "Big 'Cap." America's first $100,000-added race, it was inaugurated during the Great Depression and quickly became one of the highlights of winter racing in North America, featuring many standout competitors and storied races.

With Affirmed now clicking on all cylinders, Barrera's concern had to be the weights and any new shooters. Santa Anita racing secretary Lou Eilken, impressed by the new-old Affirmed, put 128 pounds on him. He gave Exceller, back after a four-month layoff following the 1978 Jockey Club Gold Cup, 127. He also assigned 127 pounds to Tiller, a versatile grass and dirt horse coming off a strong performance in winning the San Antonio Handicap on February 18, where he knocked off the fast California-bred Painted Wagon.

A crowd of 66,477 turned out to see whether Affirmed could keep his newly found momentum going against better horses.

The answer, on a day of broken records ($8,120,422 bet on the nine-race program, a daily double pool of $573,121, and an exacta pool of $1,232,177), was absolutely, overwhelming, indisputably yes!

Off once again with alacrity, Affirmed chased Painted Wagon through a quarter in :23 and a half in :46 2/5, but went after and collared him, following six furlongs in 1:10 1/5. Pincay had the lead to himself and a machine underneath as they advanced around the final turn.

The pair made the mile in 1:34 1/5 with nearly a three-length lead, then went away in the stretch to win, ears flickering (Affirmed's, not Pincay's) by four and a half lengths in 1:58 3/5, a new stakes and track record, the final quarter in :24 2/5. Tiller and Exceller both came from well back to finish second and third respectively (Exceller dead-heated with Painted Wagon).

This was a powerful performance for Affirmed, per-haps his best ever. Pincay said he had moved earlier than he wanted to avoid possible traffic problems and then called his mount "easily the best horse I have ever ridden. He does everything so well, and right when you want it."

The push-button horse was back, and the Big 'Cap purse of $192,800 lifted his career earnings to $1,609,318, placing him fourth on the all-time earn-ings list.

Wolfson and Barrera had already decided that the colt would stay in California for two spring races at Hollywood Park, the Californian Stakes and the Hollywood Gold Cup. After that, plans were to send him back East to run in the Whitney at Saratoga, the Marlboro Cup, and the Jockey Club Gold Cup.

Barrera also said that Affirmed would likely be given a race on grass because the owner enjoyed grass racing and Affirmed's action suggested he would han-dle turf nicely.

For the moment he would get a breather, and Barrera would undergo heart bypass surgery shortly after the Big 'Cap, because of arterial blockages, not anything related to Affirmed. While the Harbor View ace and his trainer were relaxing, interesting occurrences elsewhere were setting the shape for future jousts.

Alydar, having been given five months off, was beginning his comeback effort in Florida, while another Florida-based colt, a three-year-old gray streak named Spectacular Bid, was doing things reminiscent of Affirmed and Alydar a year earlier.

Trained by the audacious Bud Delp, "Bid" was running roughshod over his opposition in the East, and when Affirmed returned to the races for the May 20 Californian, Bid had won both the Kentucky Derby and Preakness and was odds-on to complete the Triple Crown.

Talk was well underway about a meeting, even if the race had to be contrived, between the two older superstars and the new three-year-old king.

Affirmed had other business to take care of, that of beating the seven horses that were entered to face him in the $272,400 Californian.

While Barrera was recuperating, Affirmed had been perking, working five furlongs in :59 on April 10, then vanning over to Hollywood on May 8 to rip a mile in 1:35 4/5.

He would carry 130 pounds under the Californian's allowance conditions, giving away four to sixteen pounds to his opponents. One of his adversaries was a rival from Triple Crown days, the fleet Sensitive Prince, himself having set a track record to win the mile and a quarter Gulfstream Park Handicap. Also entered were Little Reb, Syncopate, and recent Hollywood stakes winner Farnesio.

This was a race — at a mile and one-sixteenth — for speed horses going around two turns, and it was a race with a lot of speed in the field. Affirmed would have to be on his toes early to avoid falling too far back.

A fresh Affirmed was even better than a race-hardened Affirmed. More aggressive than usual, he tore out of the gate and went immediately to the lead, with Little Reb at his throatlatch on the rail and Sensitive Prince in a similar pose on his outside. Here was an unexpected spectacle: Affirmed and Pincay tackling the speed horses at their own game, and beating them.

Affirmed dashed by the first quarter in :22 2/5, then

increased his margin to a length over Little Reb in :44 4/5 for the half. He put Little Reb away turning for home after six furlongs in 1:09 1/5. Sensitive Prince had already backed off by then, and it was up to Syncopate, carrying only 114 pounds, to try to mount a challenge to the leader. He got within one and a half lengths of Affirmed, but Pincay swiped his whip three times right-handed, once left-handed. Affirmed bounded away again, winning by five lengths, the mile in 1:34 4/5, the final time being 1:41 1/5.

This was a new dimension for Affirmed, not one necessarily planned, but Pincay said that after he broke so sharply he didn't want to take any chances of backing off and getting trapped. Barrera was extraordinarily pleased, having envisioned his horse being on or near the lead.

Affirmed's earnings were $1,769,218, behind only Kelso and Forego, and the rich races on his schedule seemed his for the taking, unless the Alydar of old resurfaced in the summer or fall.

Of course, there was Spectacular Bid, of whom Pincay would say, "They keep saying that Spectacular Bid is the best horse in the country, but if we were in a race together, I wouldn't want to be on any other horse than mine."

Hollywood Park management had bumped the purse of the June 24 Hollywood Gold Cup to lure Alydar west for a confrontation with Affirmed. John Veitch thought it might be worthwhile, but Mrs. Markey said no, leaving Affirmed to pick up 132 pounds and face off against nine others, among them Italian champion Sirlad. There were some solid horses amidst the rest, such as Elmendorf's trio of Text, True Statement, and Syncopate, but Affirmed, despite giving away up to twenty pounds, was the class of the pack.

Sirlad, a star on grass, was the best bet to lower his colors, racing for lessee Abram S. Hewitt, racing raconteur and author. Sirlad, a son of the American champion Bold Lad, would carry second highweight of 120 pounds. If Affirmed could overcome the weight spread, the $275,000 first prize would make him history's richest Thoroughbred, its first two-million-dollar earner.

Unlike the Californian, there was no apparent speed in the Gold Cup other than perhaps Sirlad, and Barrera told Pincay to go early. Pincay hustled Affirmed out of the gate, steered him slightly to the right to get a middle path, and then took over. Sirlad, ridden by Darrel McHargue, was alongside with Text, and Bill Shoemaker just behind the top two in third. The other seven were out for some strenuous exercise.

Affirmed made the first quarter in :23, then stepped up the pace in the next quarter to get the half in :45 3/5, Sirlad still alongside and Text clinging to him. The leaders reached six furlongs in 1:09 3/5 with the order still unchanged, but on the final turn both Sirlad and Text edged closer. As the trio turned for home, they were noses apart and driving toward destiny.

With a quarter-mile to go (the mile in 1:34 1/5), Affirmed had the barest of leads. Sirlad was hanging on tenaciously, and Text had momentum. Would the weight finally tell on Affirmed in a life-and-death struggle with two standouts running their hearts out?

Barrera had also said that Affirmed had a reserve tank, that extra bit of juice he could find when challenged in the stretch. Alydar, and others, had seen it before, and here was Pincay searching for it once again. Affirmed, as he had so often, answered the call, and Text fell away, but Sirlad hung in there. Pincay tapped Affirmed eight times in that stretch drive, and each time he got a positive response.

The margin was a head, then a neck, a quarter-length, a half-length, finally three-quarters of a length. Then they were under the wire, winners of the Gold Cup and $275,000. The iron wall had held.

The time of 1:58 2/5 was only a fifth of a second off the stakes, track, and world record. Affirmed had run his final quarter, after making all the pace under 132 pounds, in :24 1/5. The crowd of 48,884, limp with excitement over what it had just witnessed, greeted Affirmed as great champions should be when he came back to the winner's circle.

Pincay later said, "If you had to pick the five greatest horses in history, Affirmed would be right there with them. More weight will be the only way they'll ever beat this horse." McHargue echoed Pincay's sentiments: "If you look him in the eye, like I did, or come from out of it, you won't beat him. My horse ran real big, but look what happened when it counted."

The Gold Cup would be Affirmed's farewell to California. He was bound for New York to prepare for an as-of-then undetermined race. He shipped east to

Belmont in early July. Barrera said Affirmed would train at Saratoga prior to resuming his racing tour, most likely in the Marlboro Cup on September 8. There he might meet Spectacular Bid, resting after his upset loss in the Belmont and subsequent foot injury, and Bid's Belmont conqueror, Coastal.

A possible tilt at the Whitney was scrapped. Probably Barrera didn't want to win another major race and then have Affirmed's weight assignment for the Marlboro Cup go through the roof.

Barrera also continued to say that the colt might try turf, perhaps in the Washington, D.C., International in November, although he seemed increasingly skeptical about running Affirmed on grass.

On July 15, Affirmed worked five furlongs in :59 3/5, just to stay tuned up for whatever came next. However, a meeting with Alydar would not be on the schedule. Five days after Affirmed's work, Alydar went three furlongs in :34 3/5 in preparation for the next day's Brooklyn Handicap. The morning after his work, the Calumet colt showed swelling and some heat in his right leg and was diagnosed with a sesamoid fracture. The fracture was small, but the decision to retire him was sensible, if painful. Racing's greatest rivalry was now officially ended. The names of Affirmed and Alydar would never be called together again in the same race, and the sport would be the worse for it.

As racing mourned the retirement of Alydar, his nemesis thrived in upstate New York. Saratoga is a place to enjoy, the more so if its pleasures can be taken at a leisurely pace, and Affirmed had a month at the Spa, enjoying the cool evenings, green grass, and morning gallops, with a few breezes over the track tossed in for the sake of sharpness.

Barrera, meantime, was shopping for a prep race for the Marlboro Cup. New York Racing Association racing secretary Lenny Hale obliged by cobbling together a three-horse betless exhibition on August 29 at Belmont Park. The antagonists — Island Sultan and Prefontaine — were decent animals, but with Affirmed carrying 122 pounds, they were cannon fodder.

Although he had to deal with a sloppy track, Affirmed dominated the race from flag fall to finish, winning by six lengths, running a mile in 1:34.

He was ready for the Marlboro Cup.

Maybe.

With Spectacular Bid back in high gear, Coastal ready to fire, and General Assembly, a son of Secretariat, coming off a remarkable fifteen-length, track record-setting win in the Travers Stakes, the Marlboro figured to be a challenge for Affirmed, irrespective of the weights.

When Hale announced those weights, he demonstrated the highest regard for Affirmed:

Affirmed, 133 (seven pounds above scale)

Spectacular Bid, 124 (three pounds above scale)

Coastal, 122 (one pound above scale)

General Assembly, 120 (one pound below scale)

Barrera reviewed the weights, then informed NYRA and the press that, respectfully, Affirmed would decline the issue, saying he believed the spread between his horse and the three-year-olds to be too much by a couple of pounds. He thought five pounds above scale was a stretch, seven pounds unacceptable.

The writers had fun with Barrera's and Wolfson's decision. Some sided with Barrera's views while others took the approach that Affirmed would only gain stature by running in the Marlboro, no matter what the outcome. Regardless, the meeting of Affirmed and Spectacular Bid would have to wait until the

Woodward Stakes on September 22 or the Jockey Club Gold Cup on October 6.

Affirmed, therefore, was munching hay and snoozing when Spectacular Bid dusted five excellent opponents in the Marlboro Cup, adding further drama to their prospective match-up.

When the Woodward entries were made, Affirmed was facing Coastal, Jerome Handicap winner Czaravich, older star Mister Brea, and Hollywood Gold Cup nemesis Sirlad. Spectacular Bid was absent, supposedly bothered by a fever.

The weight-for-age Woodward has been a championship-caliber test since its creation in 1953, often pitting good older horses against top three-year-olds for the first time. Scale weight conditions convey no advantages on anyone, and the race is often a legitimate test of class, bestowing upon its winner an opportunity for greater laurels at year's end.

The twenty-sixth running of the Woodward would do its predecessors proud, for there was one certain champion in this sparkling small field, and he would add yet another glowing page to his personal history.

Mister Brea took the early lead as Affirmed dropped

in behind him, only to watch both Czaravich and Coastal go by him at the half-mile pole as they decided to grapple with Mister Brea, who set moderate early fractions (:24, :47 3/5, 1:11 4/5). Onlookers wondered briefly whether Affirmed, about three lengths off that slow pace over a sloppy track, might not have his torch lit after he let the three-year-olds go by.

He quickly extinguished those concerns with a quick burst of acceleration coming off the sweeping final turn at Belmont, reaching the mile in 1:36 1/5 and extending his lead to three lengths over Czaravich by the stretch call. Coastal, who passed Czaravich in the final furlong, held Affirmed evenly, but could not cut into his margin by more than a few feet.

If his tactics gave everyone pause, the result did not; Affirmed finished the mile and a quarter in 2:01 3/5 with two and a half lengths to spare over the capable and resolute Coastal. Wolfson said that after the Gold Cup his horse would work on the turf and could go on to New York's Turf Classic or Laurel's International. Barrera was noncommittal.

The Gold Cup, of course, was what really mattered, a summit meeting between the Triple Crown winner of

1978 and the Triple Crown race winners of 1979, Spectacular Bid and Coastal.

The Gold Cup, like the Woodward, is a race of routine championship implications. Run over two miles from 1921 until 1976, it was shortened to a mile and a half to make it more competitive, an American version, on dirt, of France's Prix de l'Arc de Triomphe. The Arc, with its rich purse and richer tradition, typically attracts double-digit fields, with its winner often hailed as Europe's best horse.

The 1979 Gold Cup, with only four horses, would still be a match for most Arcs, for three of its four horses could run in any man's race. Their presence made this a memorable racing moment.

Four horses going twelve furlongs can make for a strange race tactically, especially if not one of them is a natural front-runner, as was the case with this field. Affirmed broke from post-position three, Spectacular Bid from two, a matter of little consequence going a mile and a half. In hindsight, however, it seems likely that the post positions, and the break, might have decided this dramatic event.

Affirmed was the likely pacesetter, and he jumped

away from the gate more quickly than Bid, who was sometimes a lackadaisical starter. In the Gold Cup, that habit cost him. Bid had to steady a bit after the start as Affirmed got to the path Pincay wanted, well off the rail on a drying-out track. After an opening quarter in :25 from early speed Gallant Best, Affirmed took over and set steady fractions down the backside, going :49, 1:13 1/5, and 1:37 1/5 while maintaining about a length lead on Spectacular Bid to his inside, with another one and a half lengths to Coastal on the rail. Gallant Best quickly retreated to last after his brief burst of speed.

On that long, agonizing last turn at Belmont, with Pincay holding a steady course, waiting to tap Affirmed's reserve tank, Coastal began a move on the inside that took him almost alongside Affirmed and made it appear that he, not Spectacular Bid, was Affirmed's chief threat. Coastal's bid, bold and tenacious, waned in early stretch, and Bill Shoemaker slid Bid between Affirmed and Coastal, pressing the veteran for the final three-sixteenths of a mile but never gaining much ground.

He did not give in, but he could do no more than get

to Affirmed's saddle towel, and they raced to the finish that way, Affirmed first by three-quarters of a length, Spectacular Bid second by three lengths over Coastal. The first two would become the first horses to earn more than a million dollars in a single year. The final time was 2:27 2/5, and the first three finishers were each covered with glory.

There was immediate talk of a rematch, on the grass, but after Affirmed worked five furlongs in 1:01 on Aqueduct's turf course two weeks after the Gold Cup, the talk ended. Barrera had a conversation with Wolfson, and they decided it was time to send Affirmed to Spendthrift.

As things turned out, neither of these two equine super-heros would ever do more on grass than munch on it.

It was over, the racing part that is, and the empti-ness felt when great horses retire settled in. After that uncertain beginning at Santa Anita in January, Affirmed won seven straight, notching impressive wins over the best horses in training, including another superstar in Spectacular Bid.

Competition at the highest levels takes it toll on the soundness and will power of even the finest

Thoroughbreds and it is a rare top-class three-year-old who goes one better at age four. Affirmed, though, defied normalcy in so many ways that perhaps his four-year-old ascendancy should have been anticipated. Had he merely maintained his sophomore form into the next season that would have been more than enough.

In fact, Affirmed at four was a better horse than he was at three, stronger, more versatile, maybe even more resolute, if that is possible. At the end, he was as close to unbeatable as Thoroughbreds get.

His record for the year:

Nine starts, seven wins, one second, one third, $1,148,800 in earnings.

For his career, he won twenty-two of twenty-nine races, was unplaced only when his saddle slipped in the 1978 Jockey Club Gold Cup, earned a then-record $2,393,818, and was champion of his class all three years as well as Horse of the Year twice. His presence was also the reason that Laz Barrera earned still another Eclipse Award as leading trainer, Harbor View got another leading owner trophy, and Pincay won the leading rider award.

Affirmed would fly to Lexington in late October as a

genuine American hero, a second Horse of the Year title locked up along with champion older male honors. He would be greeted by, among others, the governor of Kentucky, Julian Carroll, a man who understood that greatness in politics is ephemeral, but in horses it is enduring.

CHAPTER 9

Still A Hero

Hindsight is a wonderful thing because it allows one to be delusional without adverse consequences. It was hard, then, to blame John Veitch for indulging in a little hindsight during the long months following Alydar's injury prior to the 1978 Marlboro Cup. Veitch is an intelligent man, one whose heritage said he'd be a horse trainer, but whose life could easily have gone in other directions.

His father, Syl Veitch, said his son grew up liking horses, but was not nudged toward the racetrack by his family. In fact, when young Veitch went off to Bradley University, a school known for its basketball prowess in a place (Peoria, Illinois) not noted as a hotbed of horse racing, Syl Veitch thought his son might be headed toward a career that involved anything but horses.

Nope.

The day after he graduated, John Veitch was at the barn, ready to start life as a racetracker. Apprenticeships with his father and Elliott Burch taught him not only the basics of horse training, but also the nuances of operating in the big leagues, where the rewards are greater and the spotlight hotter.

Throughout Alydar's two- and three-year-old seasons, Veitch always seemed uniquely poised, although being in the forefront of horse racing's headline story was new to him. If he felt pressure, either as trainer of a great racehorse or as steward of a great racing tradition, he never displayed it. Reporters hanging around Veitch's barn during those years noted his accessibility, candor, ready wit, and self-deprecating manner, as well as an affinity for cats. He kept a baker's dozen or so felines around his stable at all times.

Nothing, though, could prepare him for the frustration and anxiety that followed Alydar's injury at three.

Veitch believed Alydar was at his peak when the injury occurred. He felt his horse had come out of the Triple Crown experience better than Affirmed and would have proved it with an untroubled trip in the Travers. Hindsight told him that the Jockey Club Gold

Cup of 1978, with Seattle Slew and Affirmed firing away at each other through lung-searing early fractions, would have turned into a triumphal march for Alydar. This scenario was not a delusional one.

For the ultimate "we'll never know," imagine the specter of an impressive Alydar win in the Gold Cup over Seattle Slew, Exceller, and Affirmed. What impact might that have had on Eclipse award voting?

The reality of a broken coffin bone certainly changed the outlook for both Veitch and his star pupil. Alydar was viewed by most breeding pundits as the prize among the standout horses of the late seventies, and his injury led to immediate speculation as to the advisability of attempting to race him again versus the safer course of retiring him to stud.

Had he belonged to someone other than an old-guard private breeder like Lucille Markey, he almost surely would have been syndicated for a big number and sent to stud.

Offers had already been made for him despite Calumet's history of retiring its best male performers to stud duties at the farm. The Phipps family offered to buy fifty percent of him in the summer of his three-year-old year. Mrs. Markey, however, declined, largely because the nature of Calumet's financial structure made it more practical to stand him at Calumet and sell seasons on the open market.

Consideration was given to sending him home in the days after the injury. After all, other than beating Affirmed squarely and definitively, he had nothing else to prove. He had been precocious at two, with a good turn of foot, and better still at three. He had been better around two turns than one, and he had stayed as far as American Thoroughbreds have to, in as good company as any horse could face.

He was game and willing. He was possessed of a superior racing temperament and until his injury was as sound as good horses get. His pedigree brimmed with quality stakes performers on both sides, a sales catalog writer's dream. His male line was emerging as a major force in international racing, and his female family was one of the gemstones of the *American Stud Book*.

The veterinarians who worked on Alydar following his injury told Veitch that with suitable rest and reasonable luck, the colt should be able to return to the races by late winter or spring and should be capable of performing at his accustomed level of excellence.

That thought, or hope, and the prospect of getting another crack or two or three at Affirmed, were enough to cause Mrs. Markey to concur with the vets and Veitch on Alydar's immediate future. He would stay with the racing stable and recuperate, then start conditioning for his eventual return to afternoon competition.

Veitch took it slowly, almost agonizingly so, with Alydar. The colt stood in his stall for weeks. Afterward, he walked and grazed for limited periods before going back to the track. There he cantered under a stranglehold before commencing light gallops late in the year.

X-rays told the vets and Veitch that Alydar had healed properly and completely, with no sign of any problem near the area of injury. Still, Veitch kept the powerful son of Raise a Native under the wraps, not expecting to race him until late spring or even summer. His distant goal, if it could be called one, was the Handicap Triple Crown in New York (the Metropolitan, Suburban, and Brooklyn handicaps, beginning with the Met on Memorial Day).

Alydar's first breeze was on February 26, 1979, at Hialeah, when he hauled Jorge Velasquez through three furlongs in :36 2/5. Even then, Veitch talked of a summer comeback, telling writers that Alydar might not race until July.

Alydar himself sped up the process by working so well that Veitch couldn't keep him penned up much longer. He finally unleashed the four-year-old Alydar on March 31 in a seven-furlong allowance race written for his horse. The conditions called for four-year-olds and up that had not won two races since August 20 (the 1978 Travers was run on August 19) other than maiden, claiming, or starter.

Facing five starters, two of which were actually giving him weight under the race's conditions, Alydar and Velasquez, off at 1-10, took an afternoon stroll beginning at 2:33 p.m. and ending a minute and 22 2/5 seconds later.

The big guy, burlier and more physically intimidating than ever, was scarcely out of a hard gallop the entire race, cruising along in fourth place until the far turn, when he surged forward to take control of the race, running off to a seven-length win in excellent time over a deceptively deep track charted as fast.

Veitch loved what he saw, until Alydar left the detention barn an hour or so after the race. To his dismay, the colt was lame, very lame, in his right foreleg.

He was immediately X-rayed (both front feet and knees) and then "tubbed" in warm water.

The X-rays proved negative, and Veitch decided Alydar had stepped on a stone and developed a bruise, a sensitive but minor injury. The colt was walking soundly the next day and back in training on schedule, preparing for a date at Oaklawn Park on April 13. He would face tougher opponents and carry much more weight in the Oaklawn Handicap.

Alydar and his favorite of Veitch's cats, Sparky, shipped to Oaklawn where he was to meet six opponents, including recent Fair Grounds stakes winner A Letter to Harry and another Hialeah shipper, the well-bred, Greentree Stable-owned San Juan Hill. A lightly raced four-year-old son of the brilliant Hoist the Flag, San Juan Hill was coming off an impressive victory at Hialeah and was carrying only 114 pounds to 127 on Alydar and 125 on A Letter to Harry.

San Juan Hill was relatively friendless at 11.20-1, while Alydar was 3-10. The race would come down to those two. Local favorite Chop Chop Tomahawk set the early pace, with San Juan Hill in close pursuit and Alydar just behind him through pedestrian fractions (:24 1/5, :48 1/5, 1:13).

Moving into the stretch, San Juan Hill took over, and Alydar began his drive on the rail. He was alongside San Juan Hill from the furlong pole to the wire, slowly nibbling at the Greentree colorbearer's margin, but eventually falling short by a diminishing nose, final time for the mile and one-sixteenth race being 1:43 3/5.

The result was disappointing to his Calumet connections and the crowd of 52,368 at Oaklawn, but could hardly be regarded as a setback for a horse still getting his legs back under him.

Alydar had been training and racing with a bar shoe on his left front foot since his coffin-bone injury. The bar shoe, a shoe that contains an extra piece of steel between the heels, offered some protection to the foot and ankle joint, but also might have inhibited Alydar's stride and his attitude toward racing. (Veitch said later, "I might have been too protective of him. Maybe the bar shoe made him too tentative, affected his confidence.")

Still thinking Handicap Triple Crown, Veitch then sent Alydar to Belmont Park, where he would train, bar shoe and all, for the Carter Handicap at Aqueduct on May 5, Kentucky Derby Day.

The Carter is well established as one of racing's most

venerated sprint races, an important race on its own merits, as well as a prep for the Metropolitan Handicap — a.k.a. Met Mile — on Memorial Day.

At seven furlongs, and virtually always a showcase for quality speed horses, the Carter seemed an unlikely place for Alydar to get his first stakes win of the year, but Veitch thought his race at Oaklawn was good and wanted to sharpen him for the one-turn Met, which is often more of an elongated sprint.

Alydar would be joined by 1978 co-champion sprinter Dr. Patches, multiple New York stakes winner Vencedor, the ever-dangerous and unpredictable Sensitive Prince, Island Sultan, and five-time stakes winner Star de Naskra, a Maryland-bred shipper who had finished third to Affirmed and Alydar in the long-ago Laurel Futurity of 1977.

The weights were reasonable: Alydar and Sensitive Prince, favored at 9-10 to the former's 3-2, would carry 126 pounds; Vencedor, 123; Star de Naskra and Dr. Patches, 122; and Island Sultan, 113.

Jeff Fell sent Star de Naskra winging away from the gate and down Aqueduct's backstretch in a big hurry, getting the opening quarter in :22 4/5, the half in :45 1/5.

Sensitive Prince was in close pursuit, with Alydar third but well back. Alydar started a sweeping move on the far turn, but Star de Naskra had opened up a six-length advantage before Alydar found his best gear.

The Calumet colt was charging hard through the final furlong, but Star de Naskra had enough left to hold him off by a neck in 1:21 4/5. The winner was a bit of a surprise, but would go on to champion sprinter honors at year's end. Alydar had certainly run a more than creditable race over a distance much too short for him, at least in graded stakes company.

The Met was next. Alydar's races to that point suggested that he was improving each time, a good thing going into what is invariably a very competitive race.

His opposition would include Dr. Patches again, San Juan Hill, 1978 Brooklyn Handicap winner Nasty and Bold, and a C.V. Whitney-bred and -owned four-year-old named State Dinner. A lightly raced son of the great Buckpasser, State Dinner was coming off an impressive win in Hollywood Park's Century Handicap on grass, the surface he'd sparkled over in his two most recent outings. The question of what he was doing in a one-turn mile race on dirt apparently occurred to the 50,504 in attendance, for they sent him off at nearly 30-1.

Dr. Patches went to the lead at the break, with Roman Missile and Alydar just behind him. Alydar was showing much more early speed than normal. He made a run at the leader on the final turn, but instead of sustaining his bid, he unaccountably fell back, eventually finishing sixth, more than twelve lengths behind the impressive winner, State Dinner. The Met marked Alydar's first off-the-board finish since his initial race. Yes, Alydar was conceding eight to fifteen pounds to his competition, including eleven to the winner, but this was a bad race from a great horse. Veitch said later, "It was a mistake to run him a mile at that stage in his career."

Still, coming off a strong effort in the shorter Carter, Alydar's race just didn't make sense.

Veitch was perplexed, but the horse bounced back from the Met quickly and showed no sign of ill health. The trainer was, however, not happy with Velasquez' ride in the Met, feeling he should have kept Alydar further off the fast early pace (:22 4/5, :45). He replaced Velasquez with Jeff Fell for the colt's next race, the Nassau County Handicap at nine furlongs on June 17.

This race would be closely watched by New York racing

writers, and not just because it was the local prep race for the July 4 Suburban. Many felt Alydar had been showing steady progress since his return in March, always a race behind but getting more competitive with each start.

They, like the fans who made him 2-5 in the Met, were stunned by the result of that race, or at least Alydar's backsliding performance, and saw the Nassau County as the real test of his racing viability.

A crowd of 37,619, also wondering whether their favorite son still had what it took, showed up for the Nassau County. They made Alydar a 2-5 choice over Nasty and Bold and Met Mile third-place-finisher Sorry Lookin, in what became a three-horse field after four scratches. A rainy deluge that left the track sloppy induced these defections, which included the classy filly Waya and Darby Creek Road.

Veitch, for the only time that year, had pulled the bar shoe off the left fore and replaced it with a steel shoe with clips.

It could have been the shoe change, it could have been the slop, it could have been the three-horse field or the jockey change. Whatever it was, the Nassau County saw the old Alydar, the real deal.

159

Running well off the rail behind Nasty and Bold's good pace (:23 3/5, :46, 1:09), Alydar carried Fell to the front on the stretch turn and drew away to a three and three-quarters length win, passing the mile in 1:33 3/5 and finishing in 1:46 3/5.

Finally, Alydar's fans — and Veitch — had something to crow about. The sighs of relief were heard well west of the Hudson River after the race, and Veitch began to talk more confidently about the Suburban, the Brooklyn, and what might follow (Saratoga and the Whitney).

The Suburban was, for a long time, the most prestigious handicap in America, and its ninety-third running on July 4, 1979, figured to add luster to the race's glamorous history.

State Dinner would be on hand for the one and a quarter-mile test, along with the versatile and capable Tiller, the rejuvenated Alydar, Mister Brea, and Western Front. Alydar and Tiller would be co-high-weights, carrying 126, with Mister Brea at 120, State Dinner at 118, and Western Front at 113.

Fell remained aboard Alydar, and Velasquez was named as a race-day substitute for an ill Chris McCarron on State Dinner.

The race turned out to be entertaining and highly contentious. Mister Brea took the lead from Western Front and Alydar, with State Dinner trucking along in fourth place behind a slow pace (:25 3/5, :49 2/5, 1:13 3/5).

The three leaders were almost abreast early in the stretch, with State Dinner rolling on the outside. Alydar was tenacious, but could not get by Mister Brea, much less hold off the fast-moving State Dinner, who would get the nod by a half-length, with Mister Brea another three-quarters of a length in front of Alydar.

Again, a good but not quite Alydar-like race.

Nevertheless, Veitch persevered, planning to send Alydar back in the Brooklyn at one and a half miles on July 21, although he gave thought to passing that race and going to the Whitney instead.

Following his standard procedure, Veitch sent his prized colt out for a three-furlong work on the Friday morning prior to the race, which he accomplished in :34 3/5. A win in the Brooklyn would have put Alydar over the million-dollar mark in career earnings, but he did not get the chance.

Early on race day he was found to have a puffy right hind ankle, which X-rays revealed to contain a hairline fracture of the outside sesamoid. It wasn't regarded as terribly serious, and it would have healed by late fall. However, Veitch and Melvin Cinnamon, after talking about the possibility of a return, decided it was time to send Alydar home to Calumet for good.

His career was over, and with it the official end to the Affirmed-Alydar saga. The ending was sadly anticlimactic, a whimper to end a frustrating, bittersweet year.

Veitch says now that he was probably too tentative with Alydar after his initial injury. "I never felt the confidence that I felt with him as a three-year-old. Maybe it was me; maybe it was half me, half him.

"He was like my child. I wanted to help him with his problem. You always say, 'What if?' "

Alydar left racing behind with fourteen wins in twenty-six starts, nine seconds, one third, two out-of-the-money finishes, and $957,195 in earnings. He finished behind Affirmed eight times in ten tries, but four of those losses were by a neck or less. His two actual victories over Affirmed were by open daylight (three and a half and one and a quarter lengths).

He had almost done it all, just missing in the Triple Crown and in the year-end championship tallies, surely one of the best horses never to win a divisional title. Perhaps most important was his reputation among horsemen, who would always mention his name in the same sentence with those other greats of the seventies, Secretariat, Forego, Seattle Slew, Affirmed, and Spectacular Bid.

Veitch would leave Calumet not long after Mrs. Markey's death in 1982 and train successfully for the John Galbreath family's Darby Dan Farm for several years. He would then train a public stable for a while, as well as doing occasional commentary for racing telecasts.

In a moment of sweet irony, Veitch would be hired by current Calumet owner Henryk de Kwiatkowski in 2000 to revive the stable's racing fortunes. With time, and some luck, Veitch may have the devil's red-and-blue silks back in the foreground of the nation's best races, but he is unlikely to see again a horse under his shed row able to match strides with the one that gave Lucille Markey a final glimpse of horse racing glory.

CHAPTER 10

Alydar: Turning The Tables

The most celebrated rivalry in American racing history ended with Alydar's injury before the Brooklyn Handicap. In reality, though, it had ended the year before, after the Travers, when Alydar suffered his first career injury, one that seemed to compromise him as a racehorse thereafter.

Alydar might have been reluctant to extend himself fully during his comeback attempt. Perhaps he remembered the injury or felt sensitivity in the healing ankle. The bar shoe might have been an inhibitor, although Veitch's use of it was understandable. Whatever the cause, Alydar's four-year-old season was an anticlimactic disappointment.

He wasn't far below his previous form, but the surge of power, the burst of acceleration that had overwhelmed every foe save one, was missing. It was of little solace to his many admirers that he was the best horse, at the weights, in his losses.

His reputation, though, and his prospects at stud seemed scarcely tarnished by his modest four-year-old accomplishments. Alydar was clearly going to be popular with virtually every major breeder, whether commercial or private.

He was the complete package, or about as close as a horse can get. He was by a brilliant stallion, one whose sons were already showing signs of success at stud. Albeit more noted for its distaff stars and not as a "sire" family, his female line, one of the most power-packed in the *American Stud Book*, was littered with black-type performers.

Alydar the racehorse was a soup-to-nuts standout, a high-class two-year-old who handled sprints or routes with ease, then matured into a formidable presence in the prestigious two-turn races that divide the best from the rest. He had speed, acceleration, stoutness, a great competitive attitude, and a perfect training and racing temperament.

His racecourse class was unquestioned. Whether he would have won the American Triple Crown in the absence of Affirmed is a moot question; that he was of Triple Crown-winning ability and character, there is no doubt.

Physically, he always seemed to loom above Affirmed, although the two were very similar in the common measurables: height, girth, width of chest, etc. Alydar was a robust, muscular, almost massive horse who looked more masculine than Affirmed.

The Calumet homebred would return to his birthplace under the sole ownership of his breeder. Mrs. Markey had earlier elected not to sell a portion of him because of the need to generate cash for Calumet's extensive operation, and upon his retirement she decided not syndicate him. Her decision went against the prevailing practice with horses of his caliber, but delighted the many commercial breeders who did not wish to tie up capital in stallion shares.

After some debate with Melvin Cinnamon, she decided to set Alydar's initial stud fee at $40,000, not inexpensive, but considerably under that of Secretariat (then at $80,000), Seattle Slew ($150,000), Northern Dancer ($125,000), and Affirmed, who would start at $100,000.

The price of those narrow Triple Crown losses? With his pedigree and appearance, a Triple Crown-winning Alydar would easily have commanded $125,000 or more from the outset and, likely, six figures or close to it with wins in two of the three classics.

His first book of mares was as sterling as one would expect. He got thirty-five named foals from matings to such matrons as Champagne Woman, Amerigo Lady, Bebopper, Katonka, Lassie Dear, Masked Lady, Alma North, Best in Show, Northernette, Sarsar, Kittiwake, Lady Love, College Bold, Eyeshadow, and Courtly Dee.

Nineteen members of that crop won races during their careers, including four that won stakes and six that were stakes-placed. This was a good, but not as good as expected, start for a highly touted stallion prospect and might have occasioned little excitement but for two of the crop's female members whose race records established a pattern that would become the hallmark of their sire's stud career.

The first was Althea, a chestnut filly out of the Never Bend mare Courtly Dee. She won five of her nine starts as a two-year-old, including four stakes. Among her stakes wins were the grade II Hollywood

Juvenile Championship and the grade II Del Mar Futurity, both over males.

At three she captured the Las Virgenes and grade I Santa Susana stakes at Santa Anita, was second in the grade I Fantasy Stakes at Oaklawn Park, and then came back to beat males in the grade I Arkansas Derby.

This was enough to make her slight favorite for the Kentucky Derby, where trainer Wayne Lukas opted to send her, instead of to the Kentucky Oaks. She set fast early fractions in the Derby, but tired badly in the stretch and was well beaten. Having been named champion two-year-old filly of 1983, she would retire with eight wins, seven in stakes (six graded), and $1,275,255 in earnings.

Just behind Althea in the power charts was the majestic bay filly Miss Oceana, a Woody Stephens-trainee who some felt was the better of the two as juveniles. Miss Oceana won five of six starts at two, including three grade Is, the Arlington-Washington Lassie, Frizette, and Selima stakes.

The lanky daughter of Kittiwake was also impressive at three, winning six stakes, including three more grade Is: the Acorn Stakes, Maskette Stakes, and

Gazelle Handicap. She was also second in four grade Is and completed a nineteen-race career with eleven wins, nine of them stakes (six grade Is), and $1,010,385 in earnings.

With his first crop Alydar showed he could sire stakes winners, but, more importantly, in Althea and Miss Oceana he had demonstrated that he could get the big racehorse, one capable of winning at the highest levels of competition. Nothing is more prized in stallions than the ability to get "the big horse."

The numbers were bigger in every way in his next crop, foals of 1982, and if the first crop forecast Alydar's prospects, the class of '82 established him as a world-class sire. From sixty named foals, he had twelve stakes winners, including the flashy Saratoga Six, an expensive yearling purchase who won his first four races at two, including the grade II Hollywood Juvenile Championship Stakes and the grade I Del Mar Futurity, then suffered a near-fatal breakdown that prematurely ended his career.

Another good juvenile from this group was Alydar's Best, a filly who would win France's premier two-year-old race, the group I Grand Criterium. She would win the group II Pretty Polly Stakes at three and finish second in the group I Irish Oaks and the grade I Yellow Ribbon Invitational Stakes at Santa Anita. All her starts were on turf; all her wins were at a mile or beyond.

The star of the bunch, without question, was the talented, if somewhat unlucky, Turkoman, who only started once at two. He began to show graded stakes class in the summer of his three-year-old year. He won one stakes race at three, the grade III Affirmed Handicap at Hollywood Park, but finished second in the grade I Swaps and Travers stakes, and third in the grade I Breeders' Cup Classic.

At four he was the best older horse in the land, winning the grade I Marlboro Cup Invitational and Widener handicaps, and the grade II Oaklawn Handicap, plus seconds in the Breeders' Cup Classic and Jockey Club Gold Cup. A win in either of the latter two races would likely have made him Horse of the Year; as it was, he was voted champion older male. Possessed of a long, strong run like his sire, he relished distances and earned most of his $2,146,924 around two turns.

Later maturity was a theme with this group, expressed not only in Turkoman, but also in the top filly Endear. She did her best racing at four when she won two stakes, including the grade I Hempstead Handicap, and was second or third in seven others, five of them grade Is. Another late developer who showed stakes form at three and got better at four and five was the colt Red Attack, who won or placed in nine stakes at those ages and earned $675,708 in a five-season career.

Two other males of merit appeared in this crop, and both did their best work as four-year-olds. Jeblar was Florida-based through much of his career and won four stakes at Calder Race Course at age four. In fact, all of his eleven stakes wins or placings were at that Miami track, where he was tough on the grass. Buckley Boy, a son of the good race mare Plankton, won four stakes at four, three at Calder, and the grade II Gallant Fox Handicap at Aqueduct. He went well on grass or dirt, especially over longer distances.

Ironically, 1982, the foaling year for Alydar's second crop, would also herald a changing of the guard at Calumet Farm and the beginning of a strange and frantic journey marked by both great success and, at the end, catastrophe.

Lucille Markey, her eyesight gone and her body failing, died of bronchial pneumonia in Miami on July 24, 1982. The first foals by Alydar were yearlings, but she never saw any of them and knew of their presence and promise only through the words of Veitch, Melvin Cinnamon, and the devoted farm secretary, Margaret Glass.

By the terms of Warren Wright Sr.'s will, Calumet was hers to operate as long as she lived, then would pass to their son, Warren Wright Jr., or to his heirs in the event he died before his mother. That, in fact, happened when Warren Wright Jr. died in May of 1978. He and his mother had been estranged for many years (she did not attend his funeral), and she had virtually no contact with his wife or children, leaving them nothing from her own considerable estate.

The control of Calumet did eventually fall to the heirs to Warren Wright Jr.'s trust: his wife, Bertha, and their four children. They turned Calumet over to horseman J.T. Lundy, husband of Cindy Wright Lundy, one of Warren Wright Jr.'s children. Lundy was a logical enough choice since he was the only immediate family member with any racing industry experience.

Soon, the key Calumet employees — Cinnamon, Glass, Veitch — would be gone and the farm would be in the hands of Lundy's hirelings and cronies.

For Alydar this didn't mean a great deal, since he was already a hot commodity with breeders. It would eventually lead to very large books of mares, partly because Lundy couldn't say no to the friends and wheeler-dealers surrounding him, but mostly because the farm needed the cash flow that Alydar generated.

Alydar's 1983 foals were not as notable on the racetrack as the previous year's class but included two smashing distaffers. One was the hard-luck Clabber Girl. Winner of a maiden race at two, she finished her three-year-old campaign with a reputation as a good allowance-level filly who might, with luck, win a stakes race or two somewhere along the way.

As with many of Alydar's best, she improved significantly at four and five. She won or placed in fifteen stakes, with firsts in the grade I Top Flight and grade II Chula Vista handicaps and seconds in such high-rent races as the Breeders' Cup Distaff and Ruffian Handicap.

Always competitive and consistent, she was in the

top three twenty-six times in thirty-nine starts, earning $1,006,261 in a four-year career.

The other good filly in the 1983 crop was I'm Sweets, who was classy at two, three, and four, winning graded stakes all three years, among them the grade I Demoiselle and the grade II Ballerina and Gardenia stakes. Effective at sprint or middle distances, she earned $781,973 in a thirty-two-race career.

By 1986, when Alydar's fourth crop, foals of 1984, reached the races, the book on their sire was clear: like him, his progeny were often big, perhaps a bit coarse and unrefined, immature physically as young horses. But, given time to settle into their frames, they could develop into something special.

There were six stakes winners in the 1984 group, and three of them would be exceptional, one memorable.

Two fillies, Hiaam and Three Generations, did their primary racing in Europe. Hiaam was English-based and won three stakes, including the group III Princess Margaret Stakes. Three Generations raced mostly in France, where she won four minor stakes. She came to the United States for four races in 1988 and '89, winning the Atlantic City Breeders' Cup and finishing second in the grade III Chrysanthemum Handicap at Laurel and third in the Spicy Living Stakes at Rockingham Park.

The best filly in the crop, though, was the Phipps-bred and -raced Cadillacing, a daughter of the top Buckpasser mare, Relaxing. Late to get to the races, Cadillacing had the pedigree to be anything, and she almost was, winning three stakes as a four-year-old in 1988, including the grade I Ballerina Stakes at Saratoga and finishing second or third in three others.

It was, however, the colts who led this class of Alydars. There was the medium-sized, racy-looking Talinum, a chestnut who showed promise at two with a second-place finish in the Remsen Stakes, then looked like a classic prospect the next spring (1987) when winning the grade I Flamingo Stakes and finishing third in the Los Feliz Stakes and the Florida Derby.

Forced to the sidelines by injury, he would return at four to win the grade II Stuyvesant Handicap and the grade III Bold Reason Handicap, while placing in two other graded stakes and finishing fourth in both the Metropolitan and Suburban handicaps. His form might have been compromised by physical ailments, but Talinum earned $737,818 in a twenty-two-race career and would end up standing for a time at Calumet.

Talinum's star shone brightest in the spring of 1987, but it soon was eclipsed by another son of Alydar, this one a strapping, raw-boned power runner named Alysheba. He had been a tease as a two-year-old, winning only once in seven tries, but finishing second in the Hollywood Futurity, Breeders' Futurity at Keeneland, and the In Memoriam Stakes at Turfway Park, and third in the Breeders' Cup Juvenile. He had a potent closing punch and country-boy athleticism. Everyone marked him down as a comer.

He was still a tease at three, but he got more consistent as the distances grew. While he won only three of ten starts — he was disqualified from first in the Blue Grass Stakes — he made the three count. Win one was the Kentucky Derby, in which he clipped heels and almost fell in early stretch. Win two was in the Preakness. Win three was in the million-dollar grade I Super Derby at Louisiana Downs. A narrow loss to Ferdinand in the Breeders' Cup Classic kept him from being Horse of the Year; nevertheless, he earned more than $2.5 million for the year and was named champion three-year-old male.

As a four-year-old, Alysheba finally got it all together, winning seven of nine starts and $3.8 million.

He took home first-prize money in six grade Is — the Breeders' Cup Classic, Santa Anita Handicap, Woodward Handicap, Meadowlands Cup, Charles H. Strub Stakes, and the Iselin Handicap — plus the grade II San Bernardino Handicap.

He gave away weight, proved he could handle a wet track, won with and without Lasix, and was named champion older male and Horse of the Year. He retired with earnings of $6,679,242, making him the all-time leading money earner, and with a reputation as perhaps the best American racehorse since Spectacular Bid.

Like many Alydars, he was better with maturity, although he showed ability early. Was he, as some suggested, a superior version of his sire? Alysheba earned far more money than Alydar and won two classics, but he was not as good at two or three, was less consistent, and never faced a horse of Affirmed's ability. Our vote would go to the father.

Alydar's next crop, foals of 1985, was large but not

especially distinguished, featuring five stakes winners, three of whom won minor stakes. The filly Charmante won a listed stakes in Ireland, while Lucky So n' So won Ak-Sar-Ben's grade III Juvenile Stakes and Darling Misty won a listed stakes in France.

The colt Sarhoob won the group II Prix Eugene Adam in France, was second in the group II Prix Guillaume d'Ornano and third in the group II Prix Niel, then second in the grade II Arcadia Handicap at Santa Anita.

For a while he appeared to be the best of a modest bunch, until the surprising development, at age five, of the Calumet-bred and -owned Criminal Type.

Out of the fast No Robbery mare Klepto, Criminal Type raced initially in France, winning one time in five starts and earning $14,184. He showed better form in the United States in 1989 as a four-year-old, winning two of eight starts, with five other in-the-money finishes, and earning $66,800. He gave little hint of what was to come.

Finally, he woke up in the winter of his five-year-old season, winning the grade II San Pasqual and San Antonio handicaps, then finishing second in the grade

I Santa Anita Handicap and grade II San Bernardino Handicap.

Criminal Type had clearly moved up in class, and he would show how much over the next three months. He ripped off consecutive grade I wins in the Pimlico Special, Metropolitan Handicap, Hollywood Gold Cup, and Whitney Handicap.

In a year when consistency was hard to come by, he was a standout. At year's end his seven wins in eleven starts and $2.27 million in earnings were enough to make him champion older male and Horse of the Year.

Criminal Type also represented something else: Calumet's last measure of glory linked to the old empire. His success would lead to Calumet's choice as breeder of the year, meaning that J.T. Lundy would walk to the podium in San Francisco at the Eclipse Awards dinner to receive three statues. The irony of Lundy, who was the antithesis of Lucille Markey in style and manners, accepting the Eclipse in the name of "her" farm was not lost on the audience, not a few of whom regarded it as almost blasphemous. Back home, though, the buzzards were starting to circle as word spread of Calumet's heavy debts, and Lundy was battling with the Wright heirs, who were starting to ask uncomfortable questions about his business habits.

Yet nothing interrupted the breeding machine that was Alydar. His foals of 1986 might have been his best. He sired eight stakes winners from this group, including two champions and a couple of others that came close to such status.

Atypical of Alydar's stakes winners was the Calumet-bred Joy Maker, who won only one small stakes and was third in another, but raced for ten seasons (he was a gelding and started 115 times, winning twenty-one and finishing second or third in thirty-three additional outings). The epitome of the hard knocker, he earned $239,528 in an honorable career.

More typical was the Irish champion three-year-old filly of 1989, Alydaress, who raced only at three but won the Irish Oaks and the group II Ribblesdale Stakes at Royal Ascot among her three wins in six starts. Another grade I-winning filly was Tis Juliet, daughter of the brilliant mare My Juliet and winner of the grade I Shuvee Handicap at Belmont. Beautiful Melody, like Tis Juliet, won only one stakes, but it was the grade I Beverly Hills Handicap.

Probably the best filly among the 1986 Alydars was Foresta, who garnered seven black-type wins in a three-year career, among them the grade II All Along Stakes and New York and Diana handicaps. A grass specialist, she won $639,430 and set course records at Belmont and Churchill Downs.

Alydar's stud fee had risen steadily throughout the Thoroughbred industry's rocket ride of the early eighties. Despite his large books of mares, his stud fee reached $350,000 in 1986 before falling somewhat during the industry slump in the latter part of the decade. Lundy had sold fifteen lifetime breeding rights to him for $2.5 million apiece in 1984, a figure that would hold up well even during the market decline of the late eighties.

Alydar's yearlings also sold well, but not so much to the European buyers so prominent at major North American auctions beginning in the mid-seventies. Nonetheless, he had his successes in Europe, as already noted, with the best being a colt from his 1986 class named Cacoethes.

This youngster, possessed of a powerful closing rush, won the group III Derby Trial, then finished third in the group I Epsom Derby. He followed that with a sparkling win in the group II King Edward VII Stakes at Royal Ascot and seconds in the group I King George VI and Queen Elizabeth Diamond and Juddmonte International stakes.

Cacoethes had physical problems at four, but was able to win the grade I Turf Classic at Belmont in the fall and finish third in the Japan Cup. At his best he was a top-class colt over classic distances, perhaps a bit unlucky not to have snared a couple of prestigious prizes.

Luckier, and better, was the best horse in the crop, and probably the best of all the Alydars, although Alysheba fans will always argue the point. A wonderfully made chestnut son of Relaxing, he was named Easy Goer, and he was something special from his first appearance at the track. Owned and bred by Ogden Phipps, he was one of those rare equine creatures, born to be a star and able to justify expectations.

He won four of six starts at two, including the grade I Cowdin and Champagne stakes, but was upset on an off track in the Breeders' Cup Juvenile at Churchill Downs. This defeat did not keep him from being named champion two-year-old male of 1988 and becoming a heavy winter-book choice for the 1989 Triple Crown.

At three he lived up to his hype, but, like his sire, encountered another three-year-old to be slightly better.

He won the grade II Gotham Stakes at Aqueduct in a remarkable 1:32 2/5 for a mile, then took the grade I Wood Memorial, setting him up for the Kentucky Derby, where he would be odds-on favorite.

On a wet, blustery day, he ran decently on a track he seemed not to like and finished a non-threatening second to Sunday Silence. In Baltimore for the Preakness, he got a fast track and ran one of the best Preaknesses ever, but lost by inches to Sunday Silence, who ran a literal hair better.

Back home in New York, he dominated Sunday Silence in the Belmont and then rattled off four straight grade I wins: the Whitney Handicap, Travers Stakes, Woodward Handicap, and Jockey Club Gold Cup. Facing Sunday Silence in the climactic Breeders' Cup Classic, he failed to catch his archrival by a neck, losing the race and year-end titles by that margin.

Back briefly at four, he won an overnight stakes at Belmont, was third in a hotly contested Metropolitan

Handicap, then won the grade I Suburban Handicap. Afterward, he was injured and retired to stud, winner of fourteen of twenty races (nine grade Is) and $4,873,770. He was a standout at two, three, and four, and, like Alydar, might well have won the Triple Crown had there not been another ever so slightly better horse in his path.

A race between him and Alysheba when both were at their best would have been worth traveling far to see.

The 1987 crop featured seven stakes winners, five of them fillies, and one oddity. The latter was a colt named Gypsy River who was sent to England, where he raced with modest success before being shipped off to Sweden. Perhaps it was the cooler air or the blonde beauties that got his attention. Whatever happened stimulated him to become the best older horse in Scandinavia in 1992, '93, and '94.

Back in the States, the best members of the crop were the fillies Stella Madrid, a sister to Tis Juliet, and Train Robbery, out of the terrific race mare Track Robbery.

Stella Madrid raced sixteen times in three seasons, earning $712,097 and winning the grade I Spinaway,

Matron, and Frizette stakes at two, then taking the grade I Acorn Stakes at three. She was a classy filly, a near champion at two, more precocious than Train Robbery, but not nearly as durable.

The latter raced forty-four times in four years and improved with age and distance.

Train Robbery won the grade III Honeybee Stakes at Oaklawn and the grade III Monmouth Park Breeders' Cup Handicap, among others, and placed in nine other stakes, including the grade I John A. Morris Handicap and Go for Wand Stakes. She retired with eight wins, sixteen placings, and $622,128 in earnings.

The 1988 foal crop, while possessed of several stakes and solid allowance performers, would be noted for one horse, a colt who will be remembered as one of Alydar's most talented but enigmatic offspring.

A Calumet-bred, sold privately in a package deal in late summer of his two-year-old season, his name was Strike the Gold, and by the end of that juvenile season he had only a win in a maiden race to his credit.

The early sale of Strike the Gold was typical of business inside the increasingly leveraged and cash-strapped Calumet operation. Lundy and his financial advisers were routinely packaging the farm's young prospects and selling them to pay the bills.

The spring of his three-year-old year, Strike the Gold came alive with a second-place finish in the grade I Florida Derby and then won the grade II Blue Grass Stakes. Well-regarded as a Kentucky Derby candidate, he validated that judgment on Derby Day, then would go on to finish second in the Belmont Stakes and third in the grade II Jim Dandy Stakes and the Jockey Club Gold Cup. A one-run horse, he needed a fast pace and a clear trip to put on his best show, and even then he didn't always deliver.

Generally written off as a second-rate Derby winner, he bounced back at four to win the Pimlico Special and grade II Nassau County Handicap, along with seconds in the Jockey Club Gold Cup and Suburban and Gulfstream Park handicaps.

Anything but a model of consistency, he still managed to earn $3,457,026 to go along with his big-race successes.

There were no classic winners in the 1989 foal crop, but its seven stakes winners included five graded stakes winners, among them Althea's full sister Aquilegia, who won the grade II New York and grade III Black Helen handicaps, and earned $446,081 in a thirty-start career.

Another full sister, this one to Alysheba, named Alysbelle won the grade II La Cañada Stakes at Santa Anita on her way to $355,875 in earnings.

Back at the farm, not only was Alydar one of the world's most successful sires, he was one of its busiest. At a time when the industry was in a serious economic decline and stallion books — even for the top sires — rarely exceeded sixty mares, Alydar's mates typically numbered in the upper nineties, exceeding one hundred (104) in 1989.

This figure included a number of Southern Hemisphere covers, that is, mares from Southern Hemisphere countries being bred on that hemispherical cycle, where the breeding season coincides with autumn in America.

While this practice raised skeptical eyebrows in the Kentucky breeding community, it was more and more evident that breeding rights to Alydar were being used as instruments of credit to keep an increasingly leveraged farm afloat. Likewise, starting in the mid-1980s, Lundy was breeding Alydar to Quarter Horse mares, partly as a lark but also as a means of raising cash.

The numbers — while they made breeders uneasy and led to a consistent stream of gossip about Calumet — did nothing to harm Alydar's stallion record. He had nine stakes winners from his 1990 crop, including five fillies.

The year 1990 would, however, be better remembered for another incident that would be far more meaningful than those nine stakes winners.

On the night of November 13, groom Alton Stone, on a routine security check at the Calumet stallion barn, found Alydar soaked in sweat and badly frightened, his right hind leg broken a few inches above the ankle.

Surgery would follow, and the attending veterinarians said, in effect, if things went exceptionally well, the horse could survive and possibly even breed again. Three days later, the fifteen-year-old son of Raise a Native, trying to adjust to the cast on his leg, stumbled and fell, breaking the femur in the injured leg. This time, no surgery would help. Within minutes he was euthanized, to be buried quietly on November 15, 1990, in Calumet's fabled equine cemetery.

The racing world, although conditioned to deal with

such traumatic moments, was in shock. As Calumet's financial troubles began to unfold and lawsuits and tales of Byzantine deals began to emerge, so too did rumors that Alydar had been intentionally killed for insurance reasons (he was insured for $36.5 million).

Years of legal battles would ensue, with Alydar's bizarre and untimely demise often serving as the backdrop. Officially, the story was that the horse kicked his stall door or wall and shattered his leg.

With Calumet's problems mounting, eventually leading to bankruptcy and liquidation, the insurance killing theory only grew in intensity, with a new story or rumor available from every corner of Lexington. After thousands of pages of depositions and hours of testimony, there was never any clear evidence to support the notion that Alydar's death was anything other than a terrible accident.

Federal prosecutors tried, unsuccessfully, to resurrect the case in October of 2000 during a sentencing hearing for Lundy. He had been convicted eight months earlier of intentionally hiding troubling financial information from loan officers and of bribing a bank official, including providing him with a breeding season to Alydar for one dollar. Lundy was sentenced to four and a half years in federal prison.

The ultimate irony was that the horse whose racing career had brought a Thoroughbred racing institution back to life and whose stud career sustained it would through his death be the instrument that exposed the financial miasma leading to its expiration. Calumet's collapse was the largest failure in Thoroughbred racing history.

There would be one more foal crop, and it would be a good one. There were nine stakes winners among the final Alydars, including the talented but unsound Benchmark (winner of three grade IIs at age six, seven wins in sixteen starts, $636,707 in earnings), grade III Louisiana Derby winner Kandaly, and the good filly Lotta Dancing (on the board in twenty of twenty-five starts, $358,201 in earnings).

Topping the 1991 crop chart would be Dare and Go, out of Partygoer, by Secretariat. Dare and Go was a good stakes winner in France at two and three, then improved steadily at four and five in California. He was competitive on both grass and dirt in good company, winning the grade I Strub Stakes in 1995, but it was his stunning win over two-time Horse of the Year Cigar in the 1996 Pacific Classic for which he will be remembered.

He retired with five stakes wins and eleven seconds or thirds, plus $1,608,972 in career earnings. He also provided the last glimpse of Alydar's greatness.

The stud record, Calumet's hubris notwithstanding, was impressive. Alydar sired 707 named foals in eleven crops, with seventy-seven of them becoming stakes winners, eleven percent of his named foals and fourteen percent of his starters.

His colts were marginally better than his fillies on the racetrack, but the reverse has happened at stud. He is proving to be an outstanding broodmare sire, as often happens with sires from top female families who receive good patronage at stud.

Among the many good horses produced by his daughters are Cat Thief, Secret Status, Lure, Victory Speech, Roza Robata, Peintre Celebre, Killer Diller, Lakeway, Alydeed, Ajina, Anees, Trafalger, the Australian-bred Mahogany, Aly's Alley, and Chindi. Through the fall of 2001, his daughters had produced 106 stakes winners.

Alydar was frequently among the leading sires by earnings, and he led the sire list in 1990, the year he died. He was second on the general sire list in 1988 and '89, third in 1986, '87, and '92, and ninth in 1991. At the time of his death, he trailed only Mr. Prospector in lifetime progeny earnings, and his eleven crops earned $60,604,510.

Commercially, Alydar was always popular, even with the large numbers of his offspring being offered at auction late in his career. Over his lifetime, 298 Alydar yearlings were sold for an average of $437,983. Another telling statistic is the $895,333 average paid for the seventy-five mares in foal to Alydar sold at auction.

He has not succeeded as a sire of sires, and time is running out. Alysheba failed, as did Criminal Type and Turkoman. Easy Goer had the best opportunity and showed promise, but died prematurely, and Strike the Gold, after an indifferent but not terrible start, was exported to Turkey in 2000.

There are numerous other sons of Alydar still around, but only Dare and Go seemed to have a reasonable chance to continue his sire's branch of the Raise a Native sire line. However, he died prematurely in late fall of 2001.

Regardless, Alydar will be remembered as an outstanding sire of racehorses and his name will be prominent in future pedigrees through his many daughters.

Affirmed: Steady At Stud

A lthough Affirmed's racing record was superior to that of his great rival, and although he finished in front of Alydar eight of the ten times they met, most racing men — especially those who bred racehorses for a living — believed the Calumet star to be the better stallion prospect of the pair.

Why?

In a nutshell, Affirmed had the record and the reputation; Alydar had the pedigree. Of the world-class North American equine stars of the seventies, Affirmed probably faced more high-class competitors than any other horse. Among them were Alydar, Exceller, Seattle Slew, and Spectacular Bid; of them, only Slew could claim to have a career edge.

Affirmed was the composite racing vehicle — precocious at two, the ultimate classicist at three, and a nearly unbeatable machine at four. He carried and gave away weight, handled all distances with equanimity, and possessed the courage of a lion and the constitution of a grizzly. There was never a more resolute performer, nor one of greater class. If Alydar was a heavyweight mauler, Affirmed was a sleek middleweight with a lethal, if ever-present, left hook.

In appearance he didn't fill the eye in the same way as the heavy-topped Alydar, but closer inspection revealed a substantial, almost perfectly balanced physique. He was atypical of the Raise a Native male line, although more elegant and symmetrical than most of that tribe.

Race record and appearance are two of the three vital ingredients in assessing stallion potential. It is, however, the third element — pedigree — upon which most breeders hang their proverbial hats.

There are, in truth, few successful stallions with mediocre pedigrees, in part because all other factors being roughly equal, breeders will gravitate toward sires with the best-perceived pedigrees. Since such horses get better mares than their counterparts, it is axiomatic — perhaps self-fulfilling — that they will become better sires.

Affirmed's male line was hot in 1980, in no small measure due to him, but his female family and his entire pedigree through four generations were not particularly distinguished, leaving breeders somewhat uncomfortable with his genetic make-up.

Still, Triple Crown winners that are even better older horses are rare animals, and there was no lack of interest in Affirmed at the outset of his stud career. Seasons were selling for $100,000 apiece or thereabouts when he arrived at Spendthrift Farm to join his grandsire, Raise a Native, and sire, Exclusive Native, in what was a virtual "Raise a Native" village, with the king and several of his sons and grandsons all at work.

His first book of mares was superior, with such high-class race mares or producers as Nanticious, Fairway Fable, Minnetonka, Talking Picture, Madelia, Double Delta, and the dam of Seattle Slew, My Charmer.

Affirmed sired twenty-seven named foals in that first crop, foals of 1981, and recorded four stakes winners. None were wildly successful, although the multiple Irish stakes-winning filly Easy to Copy (out of Talking Picture) was named champion miler in Ireland at four.

The Seattle Slew relative was a colt named Argosy, who won a listed stakes race in Ireland and before he could demonstrate his real merit, was injured after two wins in three starts.

Probably the best of the crop was a son of Madelia named Claude Monet, who won four of five races, including England's group II Dante Stakes, before likewise being forced to retire early.

For Affirmed, this was a reasonable, if not exceptional, beginning. By the time his next crop, foals of 1982, was into its three-year-old season, the word was not so good. Alydar was on fire, with numerous multiple graded stakes winners in his first two crops; Seattle Slew had a Kentucky Derby-Belmont Stakes winner to his credit (Swale); and Affirmed had, well, a small group of modest stakes winners.

That second crop had only two stakes winners, and the best of the duo was the filly Affirmance, who won one stakes race, four total races, and $163,211 in a three-year career.

This was hardly the making of a stallion legend, and Affirmed's shaky start couldn't have come at a worse time, with yearling prices and stud fees at an all-time high. Was the splendid son of Exclusive Native on his way to being recorded as another failed Triple Crown-winning stallion such as Citation and even Secretariat, or could he at least gain respectability?

Affirmed's next crop, the class of 1983, went a long way toward helping him achieve credibility as a sire. It contained seven stakes winners, the best of them the fillies Regal State, winner of France's group I Prix Morny over colts, and An Empress, winner of the grade III Honeymoon and Nijana handicaps and $428,895; and the tough gelding Fuller's Folly, who won Saratoga's Seneca Handicap and earned $300,201.

Interestingly, a number of his best runners were showing an affinity for a surface he never tried, grass, and his fillies seemed better than his colts, perhaps unexpectedly given that his male line contained more evident quality than his female family. And in another interesting parallel with his racetrack rival, Affirmed often sired horses that improved with age.

Affirmed's 1984 foal crop was among his best, again featuring high-class fillies along with a couple of capable males. His son Persevered won the grade II Sanford Stakes at Saratoga and a division of the grade III Hoist the Flag Stakes at Hollywood Park for Harbor View and was second or third in five other stakes in a thirteen-start career, while the tough campaigner Fairly Affirmed earned $256,970 in a long career, mostly in northern California.

The girls from that group were something special. Champion Bint Pasha, winner of France's group I Prix Vermeille and England's group I Yorkshire Oaks, and Canadian champion filly One From Heaven, winner of the Canadian Oaks and $396,376 in thirteen starts, led them. Another good female from the 1984 crop was Italian champion Medi Flash. The entire collection reinforced Affirmed's growing reputation as a turf sire.

Of the four stakes winners in his 1985 crop, three were grass horses and two of those three did their stuff in Europe. The best American was the lightly raced (by U.S. standards) Perfecting, who won the grade III La Jolla Handicap and was second in both the grade II Del Mar Derby and Will Rogers Handicap in fourteen starts in which he earned $190,869.

The filly Trusted Partner, a full sister to Easy to Copy, became Affirmed's first classic winner when she captured the 1988 Irish One Thousand Guineas, while the colt Tibullo won five stakes in Italy, among them the group I Gran Criterium. He was named that country's champion two-year-old colt.

Affirmed's class of 1986 was his deepest thus far and featured a couple of horses that came close to being the big-race standouts generally lacking in his early crops. He sired nine stakes winners in this bunch, the best being Canadian grass champion Charlie Barley. He won eight stakes in three seasons, earned $922,943, was in the first three twenty times in twenty-four tries, and earned considerable respect in Canada and the United States.

Illinois-based Affirmed's Image was durable and consistent, earning $375,364 in forty-five starts and winning five stakes. As durable, and more talented, was the capable mare Buy the Firm, who had twenty-five top three finishes in forty-two starts. She won five stakes, including Belmont's grade I Top Flight Handicap, and placed in eight others while earning $735,409, mostly in New York.

By the time Affirmed's next foal crop was on the ground, the racing industry was in the early stages of a serious market decline that would bring down, among many people and places, the venerable Spendthrift Farm. It had been built to lofty status by legendary horse trader Leslie Combs II, but destroyed by a combination of a weak market, an ill-timed effort to make it a public company, and too much leverage.

In the first great shock of the industry's depression, Spendthrift would collapse and fall out of the control of the Combs family, and its remaining stallion stars would be moved. Seattle Slew, established as one of the world's top commercial sires, would go to Three Chimneys Farm while Affirmed, in a quiet irony, would hop on a van for Calumet Farm, to join old friend Alydar.

At the stud game, at least, Alydar had the best of it, but Affirmed continued to plug along with reasonable success. However, the quality of his mates was slipping as each crop came and went without the appearance of the glamour horses so hoped for by his admirers.

The best of his 1987 crop, by a wide margin, was Zoman, a versatile and talented fellow who displayed good form at three in France, Ireland, and Italy, but really found himself at four and five.

An international traveler for trainer Paul Cole, he

won the group II Phoenix International Stakes in Ireland and the group III Prix du Rond Point in France at three, the group I Prix d'Ispahan (France), group II Rogers Gold Cup (Ireland), and group III Scottish Classic (England) at four, and the grade I Budweiser International (United States) at five.

He became Affirmed's first millionaire ($1,040,372) and was a champion in Ireland at four and five and in England at four.

Affirmed's next crop, foals of 1988, was another of his "filly" classes, with three of its five stakes winners being distaffers.

Firm Stance would win seven of her seventeen starts, among them the Top Flight Handicap, on her way to $443,774 in career earnings. Her good record would be no match for that of the superb Flawlessly, her sire's best female runner and arguably best of either sex.

Flawlessly, out of the Nijinsky II mare La Confidence, was earmarked for grass racing by her heritage. In her only start on turf at two, she won the grade III Gardenia Stakes by four and a half lengths. At three, she won five of seven and after winning the grade III Del Mar International Oaks and grade I Matriarch Stakes, would have been champion three-year-old female on turf had there been such an award.

She would have no trouble finding the throne room her next two seasons, reigning as North America's champion turf mare in 1992 and '93, winning eight grade Is during those years, including two more Matriarchs, two runnings of the Beverly Hills Handicap, two runnings of the Ramona Handicap, and the Beverly D. Stakes.

Still in great form at six, she raced only four times, but won another running of the Ramona, was second in the Beverly D., and third in the Beverly Hills and the grade I Gamely Handicap. She would retire with sixteen wins, four seconds, and three thirds in twenty-eight starts, and $2,572,536 in earnings, a daughter worthy of her father.

If the 1988 foals were good, the 1989 crop was moderate, with three decent but unexceptional stakes winners. The best was probably Abigailthewife, a late-blooming filly who found her best footing on turf, including a win in the grade II La Prevoyante Handicap, while earning $264,801.

The best male was Danc'n Jake, who raced in the Midwest with some success, winning seven races, among them the grade III Thomas D. Nash Memorial Handicap, and $245,981.

The 1990 foals featured two good fillies: one, the Irish-bred Firm Friend, who raced all over Europe in stakes company, winning the Criterium d'Evry in France; the other, grade III Modesty Handicap winner Assert Oneself, earner of $261,791.

There was a star in the crop, though, and this time it was a boy, and one who might eventually be thought of as Affirmed's best son, or perhaps his best anything.

Out of the Nureyev mare Vive, he was named Peteski, and he raced only once at two, picking up $714.

At three, based in Canada, he was king of the realm. After finishing second in the Plate Trial Stakes, a warm-up for Canada's most prestigious classic, the Queen's Plate, he won the plate itself, the remaining two legs of the Canadian Triple Crown (the Prince of Wales Stakes and the Breeders' Stakes), and the grade II Molson Export Million Stakes, Canada's top unrestricted (open to non-Canadian-breds) stakes for three-year-olds. He also ran third in the grade I Super Derby, and left the scene with seven wins in eleven starts and $1,287,864 in earnings, plus titles as Canada's Horse of the Year and Canadian three-year-old champion.

Fillies led the 1991 crop. The best was the good turf mare Lady Affirmed, out of Festivity, by Spectacular Bid. She won the grade III Athenia Handicap at Aqueduct and Belmont's Drumtop Stakes and placed in six others, earning $313,038 in nineteen starts.

Her rival for best in class was another product of the Affirmed—Talking Picture match, this one named Low Key Affair. She won two stakes in Ireland, one each at two and three and placed in two others, then came to the United States to win two stakes at four, the grade III Chicago Breeders' Cup Handicap and the Honorable Miss Stakes at Saratoga, and placed in two other graded stakes. She won seven times altogether and earned $294,159 in fifteen outings.

Affirmed's 1992 crop had six stakes winners, but 1992 itself will be noted in Affirmed's chapter of turf history as the year when he would begin a new life at what would be his final home. Calumet, like Spendthrift, was collapsing under the weight of poor decisions and crushing debt. Alydar was dead, under troubling circumstances, and the Affirmed syndicate would move the seventeen-year-old stallion to nearby Jonabell Farm in the fall of 1991. Jonabell was a family farm operated by noted Bluegrass horseman John Bell III and his children.

By now, breeders had a clear picture of Affirmed as a sire: seventy-five percent to eighty percent of his foals would start and about seventy-five percent of the starters would win. Ten percent or so would win stakes, and his starters would average almost $70,000 in earnings. All in all, he was a solid stallion, not among the best of the breed, but reliable and consistent, capable of getting the occasional championship level performer. Disappointing? Yes, considering his racing credentials, but not a failure.

All Firmed Up, a Canadian-based horse who raced six seasons, doing his best running at three, four, and five, led Affirmed's 1992 crop. He won four stakes, including the Plate Trial and Kennedy Road Stakes at Woodbine, and was second in twelve stakes, all at Woodbine, and third in three other stakes. His final record had him earning $600,670, with nine wins and twenty-one seconds or thirds in a productive career.

A more obscure but capable colt was Affidavit, who raced almost exclusively in France, where he captured the group II Hubert de Chaudenay, group III Prix Berteux, and the Prix de l'Avre in 1995 and was rated France's best three-year-old stayer, once a badge of honor but now, in the "Age of Speed," a dubious characterization.

Affirmed's 1993 foals included four stakes winners and, for once, the colts outdid the fillies. The best was probably Notoriety, who won the grade III Jaipur Handicap at Belmont and placed in three other stakes, all on the grass. He won twelve races and placed twelve additional times, tallying $423,910 in earnings.

Earning more money while winning fewer races was Firm Dancer, a full brother to All Firmed Up and, like his sibling, Canada based. He won the Coronation Futurity, Canada's premier juvenile race, and the Dominion Day Handicap, and was second in eight other stakes while earning $555,548. The other stakes-winning colt in this crop was Super Firm, who raced mostly in Louisiana and Texas and picked up $212,609 in thirty-seven starts.

The best filly in the 1993 class was Duck Trap, who raced on the Kentucky circuit. She won the Audubon

Oaks at Ellis Park and the Dade Turf Classic at the same track, with five stakes placings. In the top three eighteen times in thirty-two starts, she earned $300,011.

Affirmed's consistency as a sire was amply demonstrated in his 1994 crop, which featured two grade I winners.

The filly Mossflower, out of the Green Dancer mare Chinguetti, won all six of her races at two and three, among them the grade I Hempstead Handicap at Belmont. She placed in two graded turf stakes in 1999, and left the racing scene with six wins in eleven starts, $383,400 in earnings, and a reputation as one of the best turf distaffers in training.

The crop standout, and serious contender for his sire's best son to date, is Affirmed Success, a sprinter-miler with top form on dirt and turf. Through the end of 2001, Affirmed Success had seven stakes victories to his credit, among them the grade I Cigar Mile and Vosburgh Stakes. He had also finished second in eight stakes (three grade Is) and third in four (three grade Is), earning $1,787,895.

Affirmed Success's speed and consistency placed him among the top sprinters in the nation in 1999 and

2000 and made this late-developing horse a serious Eclipse Award candidate.

Affirmed's importance north of the border was given an added boost when one of the two stakes winners from his 1995 crop turned out to be Quiet Resolve, Canada's Horse of the Year in 2000.

Quiet Resolve stepped up in class at four in 1999, winning the grade I Atto Mile Stakes at Woodbine. In 2000 he won three of seven starts and was never out of the first three. His victories included the grade II Dixie Handicap at Pimlico and grade II Hong Kong Jockey Club Trophy at Woodbine, plus a scintillating second to Kalanisi in the Breeders' Cup Turf. His overall excellence earned him champion turf horse honors in Canada in addition to the Horse of the Year title.

Still in training in 2001, Quiet Resolve added the King Edward Breeders' Cup Handicap to his collection and pushed his total earnings to $2,063,121, while reinforcing Affirmed's impact as a sire of quality turf horses.

Three of Affirmed's five stakes winners from his 1996 crop have been fillies. The best thus far is Positive Gal, who won six of nine starts and $231,841. Her black-type outings include wins in the grade III Gallant Bloom Handicap and the Floral Park Handicap, both at Belmont.

The two stakes-winning males in the class are both turf specialists. Rhapsodist started his career in England and has won or placed in stakes in England, France, and the United States. The other is Antitrust, winner of the Meadowlands Endurance Stakes in 2000 and third in the grade III Laurel Turf Cup.

Affirmed's most recent crops, the foals of 1997, '98, and '99, are, in many instances, still racing at the time this is written, or, as is the case with most of the '99, unraced, with the foals of 2000 and 2001 yet to arrive at racetracks.

Thus far, two fillies lead those crops, the first being Tippity Witch, winner of the grade III Martha Washington Stakes at Laurel in 2000 and stakes-placed in 2001. Tippity Witch, out of the El Gran Senor mare Senora Tippy, has earned $257,006.

The 1998 filly Affluent won, in 2001, the grade I Queen Elizabeth II Challenge Cup at Keeneland, grade I La Brea Stakes at Santa Anita, and grade II Hollywood Oaks, was second in the grade I Del Mar Oaks, and third in the grade I Las Virgenes Stakes and Santa Anita Oaks and grade II Princess Stakes.

She is out of Trinity Place, a daughter of Strawberry Road, the globetrotting grandson of Nijinsky II and a successful sire. This highlights a breeding pattern, or "nick," if one prefers, for Affirmed. He has had particular success with Northern Dancer-line mares, notably daughters of Nijinsky II (Flawlessly was out of a Nijinsky II mare). At the same time, one can easily make too much out of such circumstances. It is evident when reviewing the mares bred to Affirmed in his later years that breeders took to heart the evidence of his propensity to sire good turf horses. Many of those mares had form on the grass, had produced good turf runners, were by stallions who raced on grass, or were noted for their turf winners. Thus, the Northern Dancer/Nijinsky II connection is logical and expected.

Sadly, Affirmed's life ended on January 12, 2001, at Jonabell when he was euthanized following a bout with laminitis. His death, unlike Alydar's, was quiet and dignified, the termination of a lengthy and distinguished career. He was popular with visitors, among them former partner Steve Cauthen, to the end, and he posed for thousands of photos like the celebrity he knew he was.

Affirmed's stud record is, of course, still being written on the racetrack and will be for several additional years. Barring an unexpected happenstance, however, the outcome is relatively certain.

With nineteen crops to race he has gotten seventy-eight stakes winners (nine percent of his foals) and sired runners with earnings of $43,618,008. His percentages of starters and winners to foals are typical of all stallions or slightly better than average, and his overall numbers compare well with Alydar's, except in a couple of important areas.

Alydar's average earnings per starter is $113,068, compared to $71,039 for Affirmed, and Alydar's average earning index (his progeny's average earnings compared to the breed as a whole) is almost twice as high as Affirmed's.

What does this mean?

Basically, it tells us that Alydar was a better sire of major-race winners, classic winners, or classic-caliber horses.

Both had numerous good fillies, but Alydar's males

were superior, and Affirmed will likely be remembered as something of a filly sire, although statistically his colts and fillies are about even.

As bad luck would have it, neither shows signs of being a sire of sires, although both still have enough sons at stud in the early twenty-first century for something positive to happen, particularly Affirmed.

Both have been good broodmares sires, with Affirmed's daughters producing more than seventy stakes winners thus far, including crack sprinter Big Jag, Balanchine, Lisieux Rose, Crystal Charm, Chelsey Flower, Pay Me Back, Romanov, Personal First, Pineaff, Theatreworld, Ever Lasting, and Caress.

In the final analysis, Affirmed has been well above average as a stallion, but not what one would hope for from a racehorse of his class. He was the rarest of runners, something less as a sire.

On the racetrack, Affirmed was better, if only by decibels, than Alydar. At stud, their relative ratings were reversed. Their roles as shapers of the breed are still to be determined, but the memories they left behind through their respective racing legacies will linger as long as horse racing stories are told.

EPILOGUE

Affirmed vs. Alydar — Head To Head

T o say racing never saw anything quite like their two-season war is to flatter Affirmed and Alydar unnecessarily. Separately, as well as collectively, they were great horses during one of those periods in American racing when greatness was earned on merit, not hyperbole.

There had been many notable rivalries in the past — Gallant Fox and Whichone, Equipoise and Twenty Grand, War Admiral and Seabiscuit, Alsab and Whirlaway, Coaltown and Capot, Citation and Noor, Nashua and Swaps, Bold Ruler and Gallant Man, Carry Back and Crozier, Kelso and Gun Bow, Damascus and Dr. Fager, Arts and Letters and Majestic Prince — but none had been renewed as often, as intensely, or with the stakes as high, as Affirmed and Alydar's. Their accomplishments are held in reverence, even by younger racing fans who never saw them run.

For the record, here is the chronology of their ten meetings:

June 15, 1977: The Youthful Stakes at Belmont Park
Result: Affirmed first; Alydar fifth, five lengths behind, in his first career start.

July 6, 1977: The Great American Stakes at Belmont Park
Result: Alydar first by three and a half lengths over Affirmed in second place.

August 27, 1977: The Hopeful Stakes at Saratoga
Result: Affirmed first by a half-length over Alydar in second place.

September 10, 1977: The Futurity Stakes at Belmont Park
Result: Affirmed first by a nose over Alydar in second place.

October 15, 1977: The Champagne Stakes at Belmont Park
Result: Alydar first by one and a quarter lengths over Affirmed in second place.

October 29, 1977: The Laurel Futurity at Laurel Park
Result: Affirmed first by a neck over Alydar in second place.

May 6, 1978: The Kentucky Derby at Churchill Downs
Result: Affirmed first by one and a half lengths over Alydar in second place.

May 20, 1978: The Preakness Stakes at Pimlico

Result: Affirmed first by a neck over Alydar in second place.

June 10, 1978: The Belmont Stakes at Belmont Park

Result: Affirmed first by a head over Alydar in second place.

August 19, 1978: The Travers Stakes at Saratoga

Result: Alydar is awarded first when Affirmed is disqualified after interfering badly with Alydar at the end of the backstretch. Alydar recovers to finish one and three-quarters lengths behind Affirmed.

On five occasions, the two horses finished a half-length or less apart. Affirmed won all five. The four times there was daylight between them, Alydar won twice; Affirmed finished in front twice, but was disqualified after interfering with Alydar in the Travers. Only once, in their first meeting at two, were they separated by other horses.

The margin between these two great competitors was probably best expressed in their magnum opus, the 1978 Belmont, when they were a foot apart after one and a half grueling miles, unassailable evidence of equine superstardom.

216

Those who saw it still couldn't believe. They knew they hadn't seen it before, and might never see it again. Greatness, once found, is to be treasured.

AFFIRMED's
PEDIGREE

EXCLUSIVE NATIVE, ch, 1965	Raise a Native, 1961	Native Dancer, 1950	Polynesian Geisha
		Raise You, 1946	Case Ace Lady Glory
	Exclusive, 1953	Shut Out, 1939	Equipoise Goose Egg
		Good Example, 1944	Pilate Parade Girl
AFFIRMED, chestnut colt, **1975**	Crafty Admiral, 1948	Fighting Fox, 1935	Sir Gallahad III Marguerite
		Admiral's Lady, 1942	War Admiral Boola Brook
WON'T TELL YOU, b, 1962	Scarlet Ribbon, 1957	Volcanic, 1945	Ambrose Light Hot Supper
		Native Valor, 1948	Mahmoud Native Gal

ALYDAR's
PEDIGREE

		Unbreakable
	Polynesian, 1942	Black Polly
Native Dancer, 1950		
	Geisha, 1943	Discovery
		Miyako
RAISE A NATIVE,		
ch, 1961		Teddy
	Case Ace, 1934	Sweetheart
	Raise You, 1946	
	Lady Glory, 1934	American Flag
ALYDAR,		Beloved
chestnut colt,		
1975		Nearco
	Nasrullah, 1940	Mumtaz Begum
	On-and-On, 1956	
	Two Lea, 1946	**Bull Lea**
		Two Bob
SWEET TOOTH,		
b, 1965		Pensive
	Ponder, 1946	Miss Rushin
	Plum Cake, 1958	
	Real Delight, 1949	**Bull Lea**
		Blue Delight

AFFIRMED's RACE RECORD

Affirmed — ch. c. 1975, by Exclusive Native (Raise a Native)–Won't Tell You, by Crafty Admiral — Lifetime record: 29 22 5 1 $2,393,818

Own.– Harbor View Farm

Br.– Harbor View Farm (Fla)

Tr.– Lazaro S. Barrera

6Oct79-8Bel	fst 1½	:49	1:13^{1}	2:02^{2}	2:27^{2}	3↑ J C Gold Cup-G1	3	2	1½	1^{hd}	1½	1¾	Pincay L Jr	126	*.60	83-21	Affirmed126¾Spectacular Bid121^{3}Coastal121^{31}	Driving	4
22Sep79-8Bel	sly 1¼	:47^{3}	1:11^{4}	1:36^{1}	2:01^{3}	3↑ Woodward-G1	2	2	2^{4}	1½	1^{3}	12½	Pincay L Jr	126	*.40	92-15	Affirmed1262½Coastal1203¾Czaravich1208½	Ridden out	5
29Aug79-0Bel	sly 1	:22^{2}	:45	1:09^{2}	1:34	3↑ Alw 30000	3	1	1½	1^{1}	1^{2}	1^{6}	Pincay L Jr	122	-	98-15	Affirmed122^{6}Island Sultan115^{14}Prefontaine117	Ridden out	3
	No wagering. Exhibitior race run between 7th and 8th races																		
24Jun79-8Hol	fst 1¼	:45^{3}	1:09^{3}	1:34^{1}	1:58^{2}	3↑ Hol Gold Cup-G1	1	2	1^{hd}	1^{hd}	1^{hd}	1¾	Pincay L Jr	132	*.30	99-13	Affirmed132¾Sirlad120^{4}Text119^{5}	Driving	10
20May79-8Hol	fst 1$\frac{1}{16}$	:22^{2}	:44^{4}	1:09^{1}	1:41^{1}	3↑ Californian-G1	2	1	1^{1}	1^{1}	1^{2}	1^{5}	Pincay L Jr	130	*.30	89-16	Affirmed130^{5}Syncopate114^{4}Harry's Love117¾	Driving	8
4Mar79-8SA	fst 1¼	:46^{2}	1:10^{1}	1:34^{1}	1:58^{3}	4↑ S Anita H-G1	3	2	2^{1}	11½	1^{4}	14½	Pincay L Jr	128	*1.30	103-09	Affirmed1284½Tiller127^{3}[DH]PaintedWagon115	Speed to spare	8
4Feb79-8SA	gd 1¼	:47	1:10^{4}	1:35^{3}	2:01	C H Strub-G1	8	2	3^{1}	1^{1}	1^{2}	1^{10}	Pincay L Jr	126	*.90	91-17	Affirmed126^{10}Johnny's Image115^{4}Quip115^{7}	Handily	9
20Jan79-8SA	gd 1⅛	:45^{3}	1:09^{3}	1:35	1:48	San Fernando-G2	4	3	49½	57½	33½	22¾	Cauthen S	126	*.50	88-14	Radar Ahead1232¾Affirmed126^{nk}Little Reb120^{4}	Drifted out	8
7Jan79-8SA	fst 7f	:22^{2}	:45	1:08^{3}	1:21	Malibu-G2	2	1	3^{2}	32½	32½	32¼	Cauthen S	126	*.30	96-13	LittleReb1202¼RadarAhed123^{hd}Affrmd126^{3}	Hemmed in to str	5
14Oct78-8Bel	sly 1½	:45^{1}	1:09^{2}	2:01^{4}	2:27^{1}	3↑ J C Gold Cup-G1	2	2	2^{hd}	3^{7}	4^{15}	518¾	Cauthen S	121	2.20e	65-13	Exceller126^{no}Seattle Slew126^{14}Great Contractor1264¾		6
	Saddle slipped																		
16Sep78-8Bel	fst 1⅛	:47	1:10^{1}	1:33^{3}	1:45^{4}	3↑ Marlboro Cup H-G1	1	2	22½	22½	2^{3}	2^{3}	Cauthen S	124	*.50	95-12	SeattleSlew128^{3}Affirmed124^{5}NastyandBold118^{4}	No excuse	6
19Aug78-8Sar	fst 1¼	:48	1:11^{3}	1:36^{4}	2:02	Travers-G1	3	2	2^{hd}	11½	1^{2}	11¾	Pincay L Jr	126	*.70	91-14	[D]Affirmed1261¾Alydar1263¾NastyandBold126^{15}	Came over	4
	Disqualified and placed second																		
8Aug78-8Sar	gd 1⅛	:46^{3}	1:10^{1}	1:35	1:47^{4}	Jim Dandy-G3	4	2	2^{8}	2^{7}	2^{4}	1½	Cauthen S	128	*.05	96-04	Affirmed128½SensitivePrince119^{20}Addison1146½	Going away	5
10Jun78-8Bel	fst 1½	:50	1:14	2:01^{3}	2:26^{4}	Belmont-G1	3	1	1^{1}	1^{hd}	1^{hd}	1^{hd}	Cauthen S	126	*.60	86-11	Affirmed126^{hd}Alydar126^{13}Darby Creek Road1267¾	Driving	5
20May78-8Pim	fst 1$\frac{3}{16}$	:47^{3}	1:11^{4}	1:36^{1}	1:54^{2}	Preakness-G1	6	2	1^{1}	1^{1}	1½	1^{nk}	Cauthen S	126	*.50	98-12	Affirmed126^{nk}Alydar1267½Believe It1262½	Brisk handling	7
6May78-8CD	fst 1¼	:45^{3}	1:10^{4}	1:35^{4}	2:01^{1}	Ky Derby-G1	2	2	35½	2^{hd}	1^{2}	11½	Cauthen S	126	1.80	91-12	Affirmed1261½Alydar1261¼Believe It1264¼	Fully extended	11
16Apr78-8Hol	fst 1⅛	:45	1:09^{2}	1:35	1:48^{1}	Hol Derby-G1	2	1	1^{hd}	1^{1}	12½	1^{2}	Cauthen S	122	*.30	91-17	Affirmed122^{2}Think Snow122^{3}Radar Ahead122^{2}	Driving	9
2Apr78-8SA	fst 1⅛	:45^{4}	1:09^{4}	1:35^{3}	1:48	S Anita Derby-G1	7	2	1^{1}	11½	13½	1^{8}	Pincay L Jr	120	*.30	92-16	Affirmed120^{8}Balzac120^{1}Think Snow1202½	Handily	12
18Mar78-8SA	fst 1$\frac{1}{16}$	:24^{1}	:48^{2}	1:12	1:42^{3}	San Felipe-G2	4	2	2^{1}	2^{hd}	1^{hd}	1^{2}	Cauthen S	126	*.30	89-17	Affirmed126^{2}Chance Dancer117^{6}Tampoy1181½	Driving	6
8Mar78-6SA	fst 6½f	:21^{3}	:44^{2}	1:09	1:15^{3}	Alw 30000	4	1	43½	11½	1^{4}	1^{5}	Cauthen S	124	*.20	92-16	Affirmed124^{5}Spotted Charger114½Don F.114^{hd}	Easily	5
29Oct77-8Lrl	fst 1$\frac{1}{16}$	:24	:48^{4}	1:13^{3}	1:44^{1}	Lrl Futurity-G1	3	2	2^{1}	2^{hd}	1^{hd}	1^{nk}	Cauthen S	122	1.40	92-27	Affirmed122^{nk}Alydar122^{10}StardeNskr122^{27}	Long,hard drive	4
15Oct77-6Bel	my 1	:24^{2}	:48^{1}	1:12^{2}	1:36^{3}	Champagne-G1	5	3	3^{2}	1^{hd}	1½	21¼	Cauthen S	122	*1.20	84-17	Alydar1221¼Affirmed1221¼Darby Creek Road1221½	2nd best	6
10Sep77-8Bel	gd 7f	:23^{3}	:46^{3}	1:09^{4}	1:21^{3}	Futurity-G1	2	2	2½	1^{hd}	2^{hd}	1no	Cauthen S	122	*1.20	94-10	Affirmed122^{no}Alydar122^{11}NastyandBold122^{hd}	Strong drive	5
27Aug77-8Sar	fst 6½f	:22^{4}	:45^{1}	1:09^{1}	1:15^{2}	Hopeful-G1	4	1	3^{2}	2^{hd}	1^{hd}	1½	Cauthen S	122	2.30	98-11	Affirmed122½Alydar1222½RegalandRoyal122^{hd}	Good handling	5
17Aug77-8Sar	fst 6f	:21^{4}	:44^{3}		1:09^{3}	Sanford-G2	3	2	35½	4^{3}	2½	12¾	Cauthen S	124	*1.30	92-15	Affirmed1242¾TltUp122^{hd}JtDplomcy124^{nk}	Driving,very wide	6
23Jly77-5Hol	fst 6f	:21^{3}	:44^{2}	:56^{2}	1:09^{1}	Juv Champ (Div 1) 104k	6	3	1^{hd}	1½	1^{4}	1^{7}	Pincay L Jr	122	*.40	93-15	Affirmed122^{7}He's Dewan122^{6}Esops Foibles122¾	Easily	8
6Jly77-8Bel	fst 5½f	:22^{2}	:45^{4}	:57^{2}	1:03^{3}	Great American 36k	1	1	1^{1}	2^{hd}	21½	23½	Cordero A Jr	122	4.60	93-16	Alydar1173½Affirmed122^{2}Going Investor122^{4}	No match	7
15Jun77-8Bel	fst 5½f	:22^{2}	:45^{3}	:58^{2}	1:05	©Youthful 37k	1	1	2½	2½	1^{hd}	1^{nk}	Cordero A Jr	119	3.40	90-17	Affirmed119^{nk}Wood Native119½Sensitive Nose1192½	Driving	11
24May77-4Bel	fst 5½f	:23	:47^{2}	:59^{3}	1:06	Md Sp Wt	10	1	1½	11½	1^{2}	14½	Gonzalez B	117	14.30	85-21	Affirmed1174½Innocuous1223½Gymnast122^{2}	Ridden out	10

ALYDAR's RACE RECORD

Alydar — ch. c. 1975, by Raise a Native (Native Dancer)–Sweet Tooth, by On-and-On — **Lifetime record: 26 14 9 1 $957,195**

Own.– Calumet Farm
Br.– Calumet Farm (Ky)
Tr.– John M. Veitch

4Jly79- 8Bel	fst $1\frac{1}{4}$	$:49^{2}\ 1:13^{3}\ 1:37^{1}\ 2:01^{3}$	3↑	Suburban H-G1	4	3	$3^{6\frac{1}{2}}$	2^{hd}	$3^{\frac{1}{2}}$	$3^{1\frac{1}{4}}$	Fell J	126		*.60	91-16	StateDinner118$\frac{1}{2}$MistrBr120$\frac{3}{4}$Alydr126$\frac{1}{2}$	Weakened	5
17Jun79- 8Bel	sly $1\frac{1}{8}$	$:46\ 1:09\ 1:33^{3}\ 1:46^{3}$	3↑	Nassau County H-G3	1	2	$2^{1\frac{1}{2}}$	$2^{\frac{1}{2}}$	$1^{1\frac{1}{2}}$	$1^{3\frac{3}{4}}$	Fell J	124		*.40	94-06	Alydar124$^{3\frac{3}{4}}$Nasty and Bold116^{14}Sorry Lookin113	In hand	3
28May79- 8Bel	fst 1	$:22^{4}\ :45\ 1:09^{1}\ 1:34$	3↑	Metropolitan H-G1	9	3	$3^{\frac{1}{2}}$	3^{2}	$6^{6\frac{1}{2}}$	6^{12}	Velasquez J	126		*.40	86-16	State Dinner115^{3}Dr. Patches118$^{3\frac{1}{4}}$Sorry Lookin113$^{1\frac{1}{2}}$	Tired	9
5May79- 8Aqu	fst 7f	$:22^{4}\ :45^{1}\ 1:09^{1}\ 1:21^{4}$	3↑	Carter H-G2	2	3	$3^{5\frac{1}{2}}$	$3^{8\frac{1}{2}}$	3^{6}	2^{nk}	Velasquez J	126		1.50	92-25	StardeNaskra122^{nk}Alydr126$^{3\frac{3}{4}}$SnstvPrnc126$^{6\frac{3}{4}}$	Finished fast	6
13Apr79- 9OP	fst $1\frac{1}{16}$	$:24^{1}\ :48^{1}\ 1:13\ 1:43^{3}$	4↑	Oaklawn H-G2	2	5	3^{nk}	$2^{\frac{1}{2}}$	$3^{\frac{1}{2}}$	2no	Velasquez J	127		*.30	90-19	SanJuanHill114^{no}Alydar127$\frac{3}{4}$ALettrtoHrry125^{7}	Lost the nod	7
31Mar79- 5Hia	fst 7f	$:23^{3}\ :46^{2}\ 1:10^{3}\ 1:22^{2}$	4↑	Alw 13000	5	2	$3^{1\frac{1}{2}}$	$3^{\frac{1}{2}}$	1^{2}	1^{7}	Velasquez J	114		*.10	91-17	Alydar114^{7}Fort Prevel122^{4}Jachal II109$^{1\frac{1}{4}}$	Much the best	6
19Aug78- 8Sar	fst $1\frac{1}{4}$	$:48\ 1:11^{3}\ 1:36^{4}\ 2:02$		Travers-G1	4	4	3^{2}	$2^{1\frac{1}{2}}$	2^{2}	$2^{1\frac{3}{4}}$	Velaquez J	126		1.00	89-14	[D]Affirmed126$^{1\frac{3}{4}}$Alydar126$^{3\frac{3}{4}}$Nasty and Bold126^{15}	Taken up	4
	Placed first through disqualification																	
5Aug78- 8Sar	fst $1\frac{1}{8}$	$:46^{3}\ 1:10^{2}\ 1:35^{1}\ 1:47^{2}$	3↑	Whitney H-G2	9	7	6^{13}	$4^{5\frac{1}{2}}$	1^{4}	1^{10}	Velasquez J	123		*.70	98-09	Alydar123^{10}Buckaroo112^{hd}Father Hogan114^{nk}	Hand ride	9
22Jly78- 8AP	fst $1\frac{1}{4}$	$:47^{4}\ 1:11^{1}\ 1:35^{3}\ 2:00^{2}$		Arl Classic-G2	3	3	$2^{3\frac{1}{2}}$	1^{5}	1^{8}	1^{13}	Fell J	126		*.05	95-19	Alydar126^{13}ChiefofDixieland114^{1}GordieH.114^{5}	Much best	5
10Jun78- 8Bel	fst $1\frac{1}{2}$	$:50\ 1:14\ 2:01^{3}\ 2:26^{4}$		Belmont-G1	2	3	2^{1}	2^{hd}	2^{hd}	2^{hd}	Velasquez J	126		1.10	86-11	Affirmed126^{hd}Alydar126^{13}Darby Creek Road126$^{7\frac{3}{4}}$	Game try	5
20May78- 8Pim	fst $1\frac{3}{16}$	$:47^{3}\ 1:11^{4}\ 1:36^{1}\ 1:54^{2}$		Preakness-G1	3	6	$6^{5\frac{1}{2}}$	4^{2}	$2^{\frac{1}{2}}$	2^{nk}	Velasquez J	126	b	1.80	98-12	Affirmed126^{nk}Alydar126$^{7\frac{1}{2}}$Believe It126$^{2\frac{1}{2}}$	Game effort	7
6May78- 8CD	fst $1\frac{1}{4}$	$:45^{3}\ 1:10^{4}\ 1:35^{4}\ 2:01^{1}$		Ky Derby-G1	10	9	9^{17}	$4^{4\frac{1}{2}}$	3^{4}	$2^{1\frac{1}{2}}$	Velasquez J	126	b	*1.20	89-12	Affirmed126$^{1\frac{1}{2}}$Alydar126$^{1\frac{1}{4}}$Believe It126$^{4\frac{1}{4}}$	Closed fast	11
27Apr78- 7Kee	gd $1\frac{1}{8}$	$:47^{1}\ 1:11^{2}\ 1:37^{2}\ 1:49^{3}$		Blue Grass-G1	9	6	6^{11}	4^{7}	1^{6}	1^{13}	Velasquez J	121	b	*.10	89-19	Alydar121^{13}Raymond Earl121^{no}Go Forth121$^{1\frac{3}{4}}$	Ridden out	9
1Apr78- 9GP	fst $1\frac{1}{8}$	$:47^{1}\ 1:11^{1}\ 1:35^{2}\ 1:47$		Florida Derby-G1	6	4	2^{1}	$1^{\frac{1}{2}}$	1^{hd}	1^{2}	Velasquez J	122	b	*.20	99-10	Alydar122^{2}Believe It122$^{7\frac{1}{2}}$Dr. Valeri122^{nk}	Handily	7
4Mar78- 9Hia	fst $1\frac{1}{8}$	$:45^{3}\ 1:09^{4}\ 1:35\ 1:47$		Flamingo-G1	6	6	6^{5}	3^{1}	1^{2}	$1^{4\frac{1}{2}}$	Velasquez J	122	b	*.90e	97-05	Alydar122$^{4\frac{1}{2}}$NoonTimeSpender122^{1}Dr.Valeri122^{nk}	Ridden out	8
11Feb78- 5Hia	fst 7f	$:23^{4}\ :46^{4}\ 1:10^{3}\ 1:22^{1}$		Alw 14000	5	8	5^{4}	$5^{3\frac{1}{2}}$	2^{hd}	1^{2}	Velasquez J	122	b	*.30	92-13	Alydr122^{2}NoonTimeSpendr119$^{5\frac{1}{2}}$LaVoyagus109^{nk}	Ridden out	8
26Nov77- 8Aqu	sly $1\frac{1}{8}$	$:47^{1}\ 1:11^{2}\ 1:35^{1}\ 1:47^{4}$		Remsen-G2	5	4	4^{9}	$4^{5\frac{1}{2}}$	3^{5}	2^{2}	Velasquez J	122	b	*.60	94-13	Believe It122^{2}Alydar122$^{1\frac{1}{4}}$Quadratic116^{6}	2nd best	5
29Oct77- 8Lrl	fst $1\frac{1}{16}$	$:24\ :48^{4}\ 1:13^{3}\ 1:44^{1}$		Lrl Futurity-G1	1	3	3^{1}	1^{hd}	2^{hd}	2^{nk}	Velasquez J	122	b	*.40	92-27	Affirmed122^{nk}Alydr122^{10}StrdNskr122^{27}	Steadied,sharp try	4
15Oct77- 6Bel	my 1	$:24^{2}\ :48^{1}\ 1:12^{2}\ 1:36^{3}$		Champagne-G1	1	5	4^{2}	$5^{2\frac{3}{4}}$	$4^{1\frac{1}{2}}$	$1^{1\frac{1}{4}}$	Velasquez J	122	b	1.50	85-17	Alydar122$^{1\frac{1}{4}}$Affirmed122$^{1\frac{1}{4}}$DarbyCreekRoad122$^{1\frac{1}{2}}$	Ridden out	6
10Sep77- 8Bel	gd 7f	$:23^{3}\ :46^{3}\ 1:09^{4}\ 1:21^{3}$		Futurity-G1	1	5	$3^{2\frac{1}{2}}$	2^{hd}	1^{hd}	2no	Maple E	122	b	1.50	94-10	Affirmd122^{no}Alydr122^{11}NstyndBold122^{hd}	Short lead,missed	5
27Aug77- 8Sar	fst $6\frac{1}{2}$f	$:22^{4}\ :45^{1}\ 1:09^{1}\ 1:15^{2}$		Hopeful-G1	1	4	4^{4}	$4^{\frac{3}{4}}$	2^{hd}	$2^{\frac{1}{2}}$	Maple E	122	b	*1.00	97-11	Affirmed122$\frac{1}{2}$Alydar122$^{2\frac{1}{2}}$RegalandRoyl122^{hd}	Steadied early	5
13Aug77- 8Mth	sly 6f	$:22^{2}\ :45^{3}\ \ 1:10^{3}$		Sapling-G1	4	5	3^{4}	2^{3}	2^{hd}	$1^{2\frac{1}{2}}$	Maple E	122	b	*.60	87-17	Alydr122$^{2\frac{1}{2}}$NoonTimeSpendr122$^{4\frac{1}{2}}$DominantRulr122^{no}	Easily	5
27Jly77- 8Bel	fst 6f	$:23\ :45^{4}\ \ 1:10$		Tremont 36k	4	4	3^{3}	$3^{1\frac{1}{2}}$	1^{1}	$1^{1\frac{1}{4}}$	Maple E	124		*.40	92-16	Alydar124$^{1\frac{1}{4}}$Believe It117$^{3\frac{3}{4}}$Jet Diplomacy124$^{5\frac{1}{2}}$	Ridden out	5
6Jly77- 8Bel	fst $5\frac{1}{2}$f	$:22^{2}\ :45^{4}\ :57^{2}\ 1:03^{3}$		Great American 36k	7	7	$4^{2\frac{1}{2}}$	1^{hd}	$1^{1\frac{1}{2}}$	$1^{3\frac{1}{2}}$	Maple E	117		*.80	97-16	Alydar117$^{3\frac{1}{2}}$Affirmed122^{2}Going Investor122^{4}	Ridden out	7
24Jun77- 4Bel	fst $5\frac{1}{2}$f	$:22^{4}\ :46^{1}\ :58^{1}\ 1:04^{1}$		Md Sp Wt	9	8	$6^{3\frac{3}{4}}$	1^{hd}	1^{2}	$1^{6\frac{3}{4}}$	Maple E	122		*2.10	94-20	Alydar122$^{6\frac{3}{4}}$Believe It122^{1}Sauce Boat117$^{3\frac{1}{2}}$	Handily	10
15Jun77- 8Bel	fst $5\frac{1}{2}$f	$:22^{2}\ :45^{3}\ :58^{2}\ 1:05$		©Youthful 37k	7	9	9^{12}	9^{11}	5^{10}	5^{5}	Maple E	115		*1.80	85-17	Affirmed119^{nk}WoodNative119$\frac{1}{2}$SenstvNos119$^{2\frac{1}{2}}$	In close turn	11

Copyrighted © 2000 by Daily Racing Form, Inc. Reprinted from the book "Champions" (DRF Press)

Index

223

Photo Credits

Cover photo: (NYRA-Bob Coglianese)

Page 1: Affirmed and Alydar (Jerry Cooke Collection); Affirmed head shot (Santa Anita); Alydar head shot (Tony Leonard)

Page 2: Exclusive Native (Tony Leonard); Won't Tell You (John Noye); Crafty Admiral (The Blood-Horse)

Page 3: Native Dancer (Peter Winants); Raise a Native (NYRA-Mike Sirico); Sweet Tooth (Milt Toby); On-and-On (Skeets Meadors)

Page 4: Steve Cauthen aboard Affirmed (Tony Leonard); Louis and Patrice Wolfson (Inger Drysdale); Laz Barrera (Dell Hancock)

Page 5: Jorge Velasquez (The Blood-Horse); John Veitch and Alydar (Jim Raftery); Lucille Markey (The Blood-Horse)

Page 6: Affirmed's Youthful (NYRA-Bob Coglianese); Alydar's Great American (NYRA-Bob Coglianese); Affirmed's Hopeful (NYRA-Bob Coglianese)

Page 7: Affirmed's Futurity (NYRA-Bob Coglianese); Alydar's Champagne (NYRA-Bob Coglianese); Affirmed's Laurel Futurity (Jerry Frutkoff/James McCue)

Page 8: Alydar with groom (Keeneland); Alydar's Blue Grass (Milt Toby); Affirmed at three (The Blood-Horse); Affirmed's Santa Anita Derby (Santa Anita)

Page 9: Cauthen and Affirmed with roses (Milt Toby); Affirmed's Kentucky Derby (Kinetic Corporation)

Page 10: Preakness finish side view (Jerry Frutkoff); Preakness finish inside rail (Jerry Frutkoff)

Page 11: Belmont finish close up (NYRA-Bob Coglianese); Belmont finish head on (Jerry Cooke Collection)

Page 12: Affirmed's Jim Dandy (NYRA-Bob Coglianese); Alydar's Whitney (NYRA); Affirmed and Alydar in Travers (NYRA-Bob Coglianese)

Page 13: Affirmed's Strub (Vic Stein); Affirmed's Californian (Kevin Ellsworth); Affirmed's Hollywood Gold Cup (Kevin Ellsworth); Alydar (NYRA)

Page 14: Barrera and Affirmed (NYRA); Pincay and Affirmed (Dell Hancock); Affirmed's Jockey Club Gold Cup (NYRA); Affirmed's retirement ceremony (NYRA)

Page 15: Zoman (Richard Quinn); Flawlessly (Stidham and Associates); Peteski (Michael Burns); Affirmed's gravesite (Tom Hall)

Page 16: Althea (Del Mar); Alysheba (Four Footed); Easy Goer (Dan Johnson); Alydar's gravestone (Barbara D. Livingston)

ABOUT THE
AUTHOR

Timothy T. Capps (1946–2017) has been involved in nearly every aspect of the Thoroughbred industry. During the 1970s and mid-80s, Capps served as editor of *The Thoroughbred Record*, a leading industry monthly. In the mid-80s he ventured into the high-stakes stallion market as an executive with Matchmaker, a company that sold stallion seasons and shares.

From there he was lured to the racetrack and went to the Maryland Jockey Club, which oversees racing at Pimlico and Laurel Park. After serving as vice president of the Maryland Horse Breeders Association and editor and publisher of *MidAtlantic Thoroughbred*, Capps returned to the Maryland Jockey Club as executive vice president.

Capps was the author of two other books in the Thoroughbred Legends series, one on Spectacular Bid and one on Secretariat. He resided in Columbia, Maryland.